'A wonderful account of some o
bringing Christians together thro
of their communities. Read it, be
Rev Gavin Calver, Director of Mission, Evangelism ~~....~~

'Millions pray, "Thy Kingdom come", and this book helps us see what that Kingdom looks like "on earth as it is in heaven". Written from a personal perspective, gathering accounts from around the country, this important book charts new Christian unity movements that are changing lives and transforming communities. Nothing could be more important as we work together in Jesus' name.'
Captain Jim Currin, Church Army; Head of Evangelisation, Mission, and Media at Churches Together in England

'Roger Sutton is a gatherer. A gatherer of stories about cities and about unity across the Church. A gatherer of good news examples of an increasingly amazing move of God connecting Christian leaders across numerous towns and cities. Roger is a gatherer with a clear biblical understanding of the theology of place. Read this gatherer's book to be both encouraged and challenged.'
Lloyd Cooke, Chief Executive, Saltbox Christian Centre, Stoke-on-Trent

'Unity is something we know reflects the nature of God and yet so often seems to fall into the "too hard" category on our list of things to do! As you read the stories and reflections in this book you will be inspired and encouraged to invest in nurturing partnerships for the sake of the Kingdom. If you long to see God's Kingdom come in your community, then this is a book for you.'
Rev Lynn Green, General Secretary, The Baptist Union of Great Britain

'Roger is a great communicator. Over recent years I have heard him speak several times on this subject. Now as I read his book I "hear" the same passion calling the Church to unity and mission in the communities of the land. This is such an essential message for the Church today, and this book delivers. Great stories, readable theology, practical wisdom with humour, and all couched in a passionate challenge for the Church to be Jesus in our cities and towns. Down to earth and applicable.'

Ian Shelton, National Leader of One Heart Australia, a network linking the unity movements across the nation

'Roger Sutton has given a gift to the global church by capturing a panoramic view of the flourishing urban church in the United Kingdom. What God is doing through the UK Gather Movement powerfully affirms that the New Reformation is God uniting the Church in major cities globally. Sutton's leadership is one of the many bright spots on the global landscape.'

Dr Mac Pier, CEO and Founder, The NYC Leadership Center; Co-founder Movement Day

'In *A Gathering Momentum*, Roger Sutton has captured some of the stories, the vision and the values of what I'm convinced is a God movement. When Roger joined us at the Evangelical Alliance in 2010, the challenge was simple: find out what God is doing in the towns and cities across the UK and how we play our part to see His purposes advance. None of us quite expected what he was to discover – and it wasn't just happening here; it was happening across the world.'

Steve Clifford, General Director, Evangelical Alliance

'A wonderful thing is happening all over the UK. But you won't read about it in the papers because it's not tragic or scandalous. It's beautiful, and this book throws open windows on to that glorious vista. Roger hasn't sent a team of researchers around the country to glean "good news stories". He knows and loves these people. He has built relationships with them, and through Gather and Movement Day UK those relationships are bearing fruit. I challenge you to read this book and not come away full of faith and hope for what is possible in our nation and beyond.'

Andy Flanagan, Director of Christians in Politics; singer/ songwriter

'This is an inspiring and imagination-expanding book. It not only captures the extraordinary impact that friendship, prayer and purposeful unity among church leaders can have on a town but also shows us the first fruits of what such unity among lay Christians across the sectors can produce. Bravo.'

Mark Greene, Executive Director, LICC

'The original meaning of the word *ecclesia* – translated in the New testament as "church" – can be expressed as "a group of concerned citizens coming together to discuss the future of their city". Such a definition fits perfectly with the thrilling vision of Christian unity and action offered in *A Gathering Momentum*. This is a story Roger Sutton is uniquely positioned to tell. In twenty-two years of pastoral ministry and now seven years working with unity movements in the UK and around the world, he has seen from the inside what it takes to bring transformation to the places we inhabit. Passionate in equal measure for the revealing of God's Kingdom and for the unity of the Church, Roger has discovered that sweet spot where prayer and activism meet and unity and transformation collide. The result is a beautiful account of places where the flowers of the Kingdom are breaking through the concrete of our cities. This book is more, though, than an archive of achievements, inspiring as they are. It is above all an invitation to us all to join a movement that has God's fingerprints all over it: to come together in prayer, cooperation and shared commitment to the transformation of the places God has set us in.'

Gerard Kelly, Co-director of the Bless Network

'As a local church leader in Roger Sutton's home city of Manchester, I can wholeheartedly testify to his unrelenting vision and passion for the unity of Christ's church. But this book is not merely an appeal for sentimental expressions of goodwill and understanding. This book offers evidence that something much more powerful is possible. Built on the foundation of genuine love and relationship, members and leaders can work strategically together across their churches to see more of God's kingdom come in the places where they live and work. Roger's pursuit of this dream has made its mark on my own life and ministry and I urge us all in the church to listen to what he has to say here.'

Richard Anniss, King's Church in Greater Manchester

'The Kingdom agenda has always been for Jesus Christ to be present, active and bring to Himself every part of global existence. This mandate is the marching order of the Church. Roger Sutton, has a bird's eye view on this reality in the UK like no one else I know. This book masterfully documents and communicates this reality, showing evidence of a growing unity in the church, where people are beginning to lift up their eyes towards a greater vision of praying and working for the transformation of the spiritual, social and cultural challenges of their town or city. As you read this book, you will be inspired to love God, love others, and love the places God has sent us to.'

Alan Platt, Global Leader, Doxa Deo & City Changers

'Having been engaged with citywide movements since the early 80's, I am heartened by Roger and his UK colleagues taking Jesus' highest command seriously, not with standard lip-service, but radical sacrifice. What most got my attention was Roger's dreams for Trafford, his own Burrough, his town, with its mix of troubles and treasures. A Gathering Momentum has in-the-trench nuggets to help grow God's kingdom in your parish, and trans-locally to other communities that hunger for real-deal John 17 unity. "Sir Roger" nails what we're really about in his closing chapter:"a generational commitment of sacrifice and service to a place." Movement? Momentum? Perhaps a virtual, global reformation of how we "do church." Friends...we're in it!'

Tom White, Frontline Ministries, Coordinator, Global Cities Leadership Community, City Gospel Movement National Team (USA)

A GATHERING MOMENTUM

Stories of Christian Unity Transforming Our Towns and Cities

Edited by
Roger Sutton

instant
apostle

First published in Great Britain in 2017

Instant Apostle
The Barn
1 Watford House Lane
Watford
Herts
WD17 1BJ

Copyright © Roger Sutton 2017

All rights reserved. No portion of this book may be reproduced or transmitted in any form or by any means, electronic or mechanical, including photocopying, recording, or by any information storage and retrieval system, without permission in writing from the publisher.

Unless otherwise indicated, all Scripture quotations are taken from the Holy Bible, New International Version® Anglicized, NIV® Copyright © 1979, 1984, 2011 by Biblica, Inc.® Used by permission. All rights reserved worldwide.

Scripture quotations marked 'The Message' are taken from The Message. Copyright © 1993, 1994, 1995, 1996, 2000, 2001, 2002. Used by permission of NavPress Publishing Group.

Scripture quotations marked 'NCV' are taken from the New Century Version®. Copyright © 2005 by Thomas Nelson. Used by permission. All rights reserved.

Every effort has been made to seek permission to use copyright material reproduced in this book. The publisher apologises for those cases where permission might not have been sought and, if notified, will formally seek permission at the earliest opportunity.

The views and opinions expressed in this work are those of the author and do not necessarily reflect the views and opinions of the publisher.

British Library Cataloguing-in-Publication Data

A catalogue record for this book is available from the British Library

This book and all other Instant Apostle books are available from Instant Apostle:

Website: www.instantapostle.com

E-mail: info@instantapostle.com

ISBN 978-1-909728-75-2

Printed in Great Britain

Dedication

To Lel: 'my friend, nurturer and life partner through this extraordinary journey'.

To Jim, Steve, Naomi and Sam: 'Forever proud and thankful for you.'

Contents

Introduction

This book seeks to tell the story of what God is doing across cities and towns in the UK. A movement is happening in many cities and towns where church leaders and 'ordinary' Christians are working together in unity for the sake of the future transformation of their places.

This is a collection of those stories from a network called Gather. It seeks to highlight the breadth, imagination and ambition of these extraordinary people. The book seeks to draw out the main values and lessons learned so that those who are just starting to get a vision for their places and want to work in unity to see transformation can get off to a great start and not have to repeat the same mistakes as others. This is about reflection, highlighting best practice and starting to chart the way ahead.

We would like to thank all those from the Gather network who contributed to this book; this is your story as well as ours and we hope we have been able to do it justice. We apologise if your city is not in the book – we simply did not have the time or space to include every story from more than 130 towns and cities, but we hope you will see your story reflected in others.

We owe a depth of gratitude and thanks to Steve Clifford, Krish Kandiah and Gavin Calver for the support of the Evangelical Alliance over the years. The EA has given time and resources to enabling the Gather network to flourish; it has never sought to own or control what God is doing in towns and cities, but to bless and cheer on. It has won many new friends with this kingdom attitude.

I would like to thank the main Gather team and wider supporters and friends. I am so appreciative of their support, inspiration and friendship. A big thank you to Lesley Sutton, David and Karen King, Ian Mayer, Sarah Riseley, Ewen Huffman, Lucy Olofinjana, Lloyd Cooke, Steve Botham, Andy Frost, David Dorricott, Graham Hutchinson, Stephen Sutton, Andy and Sue Glover, Tim Roberts, Brendan Munro, Paul Barratt, Chris Clewer, Debra Green, Peter Heywood, Neil Hudson, Mark Green, Sheena Tranter, Andy Flannagan, Mac Pier, Tom White, Ian Shelton, Alan Platt, Steve and Sandra Cobbin, Dave and Alison Kirby, Theresa Grant, Sean Anstee, Chris Hart, Richard Anniss, Rob White, Chick Yuill and many, many others. Bless you!

Throughout the book we have used the terms 'towns' and 'cities' to give a context for place-based transformational work. We should really use a much longer list of names that include villages, cities, boroughs, islands and regions, because the transformational vision is for any place that has a defined context, culture and geography. For ease of use we have paraphrased all these contexts into the words 'cities' and 'towns', but the movement of God's transformation is coming to any and every place!

> I will give you every place where you set your foot.
> *Joshua 1:3*

I See a New City
by Gerard Kelly[1]

I see a new city, poured out from Heaven
Dressed for a party; blazing with beauty
Her rooftops are radiant, trees trembling with laughter
And joy like a jewel shines in her streets.

From her walls and windows
No weeping is heard
Through her gateways and gutters
Floods of tears do not flow
For in her homes and houses no pain dwells
Bricks once broken down in mourning
Rise again in song and celebration
Stones thrown down by enmity and envy
Dare to dance in swirling swathes of mercy

She sings: a million voices rising
The long-lost languages of human hopes
The secret praise of human hearts, released at last
Because her God is with her
Because his home is made
Within her walls

---

[1] Used with permission.

Because his voice is heard
Gentle like the rains of spring
Declaring: New! New! New!

This is the city I see
The future I belong to
This is the blueprint my heart holds on to
Even now, in streets that sing another story
Even here, beneath a darker vision's shadow
This metropolis of mercy
Promising future realisation
Active now in Love's imagination
This is my dream
And though I wait, and though I long
And though the sacred city may seem slow:
Still I will hope
Still I will pray
Still I will today
Rise up and build.

Chapter 1
The New City

I had spent several months discussing the role of faith groups in our borough with the chief executive of the council, informing him of the wide array of services they provide, the social infrastructure they create, and the resources of volunteers, buildings and staff they offer. I was delighted when he responded so positively. I was so proud of the seventy-plus churches in our borough who serve day in and day out providing care for the elderly, shelter for the homeless, support for young people, skills development for the unemployed, parenting advice for families and much, much more.

However, then came the word 'but'. What could possibly be wrong with this shining example of charity and faith in action? What critique could he offer that would have significance for this vital third-sector activity? Then his comments hit me: he said it was impressive and laudable but not very strategic or coordinated.

I wanted to argue back and suggest it was: to defend the thought-through, planned and cooperative actions of the Church in society. But as soon as he uttered these words I knew he was speaking the truth. It is very impressive and very noble that the Church provides numerous activities and services for the community, but there is little to no coordination between churches, or strategic approaches within churches, and often no relationships or partnerships with civic authorities, private-sector or even other third-sector providers. We do our own thing in our own local churches, with little conversation about the needs and aspirations of the wider society, with almost no significant relationship with other Christian communities involving strategy, planning or cooperation. We play our own instrument to our tune in our own rhythm, often out of key and out of time with others who are playing a different melody.

One of the reasons we perpetuate this individualistic approach to ministry is because we lack an all-encompassing vision for the places we live in. We are not strategic and coordinated because we don't have to be. If all we want to achieve is to grow our church and affect a few people who come in contact with us, we really don't need to relate to other churches or civic authorities. The size of our vision is often about the church growing in numbers, hopefully by conversion, but often by transfer, or the multiplication of other churches. Those are the success criteria, the ruler by which we judge success or failure.

But the biblical picture of mission to the earth is much wider and all-encompassing. The gigantic picture of the kingdom of God coming to earth is about the renewal and transformation of the cosmos. Jesus, as it says in the book of Ephesians (1:10), is gathering together all that is broken and divided, all that is fractured and dislocated. Under Him 'all things' will be redeemed. The term 'all things' is exactly what it says – it means everything in earth and heaven. He is present, active and bringing to Himself under His authority every part of global existence.

The Church is part of this unifying gathering, and it is also at the same time the primary channel of witness to the world that Christ is bringing all things together under Him. That's why Jesus prays for the unity of His Church, not because it's a nice thing for believers to get on with each other, but because it's a huge neon sign to the cosmos that God is active in this world and His rulership is coming. If you want to get a taste of what God is about in this world, take a look at your local expression of God's people.

The Church is, then, the starting point, the sluice gate for the bursting dam of God's love into the world. This gathering love is flowing down to every part of society, every living human being, every structure, culture, institution and government. The Christian virus of the kingdom of Christ, with its core DNA of kindness, patience, justice, forgiveness, generosity, faith, hope, beauty, goodness, wisdom and above all, love, is infecting 'all things'. So it spreads across the factory floor into the habits and lifestyles of ordinary people and then into the financial and employment decisions made in the boardroom. It infects the teacher with her classroom full of kids from dislocated families and flows out into the community where these scrapheap kids begin to flourish and grow. Cultures in the health service begin to be challenged and changed, the art gallery begins to value beauty more than meaninglessness, and the local sports group grows in team spirit. Local streets begin to understand what being a good neighbour is about, the elderly are better cared for, people feel safer and have a deep sense of belonging to a place. The kingdom is rising, the floodwaters are breaking through the most resistant barriers, and Christ is slowly but surely gathering to Himself His own creation.

Abraham Kuyper said it so well when he uttered these words:

> Oh, no single piece of our mental world is to be hermetically sealed off from the rest, and there is not a square inch in the whole domain of our human existence over which Christ, who is Sovereign over *all*, does not cry: 'Mine!'[2]

Once the light goes on in our dull minds that Christ declares 'Mine!' over 'all things', we begin to realise that he may be interested in slightly more than my own walk with Him, and my own church and its ministry. He declares His ownership over the street I live in, the shopping centre I visit, the health service I access, the policewoman I see, the coffee shop I sit in, the business I work for, the energy company I rely on, the road I drive down, the garden I sit in, the bank I withdraw cash from, the internet provider I use, the local council I moan about, the school I send my kids to, the village I adore, the town I come from and the city I am a part of, and everything else besides. This is a big, wide, all-encompassing vision for every street, hamlet, village, town, borough and city across this wonderful nation and beyond.

But of course it must be pie in the sky, a flight of fancy, a wonderful utopian theology that has no real traction here

---

[2] 1880 Inaugural Lecture, Free University of Amsterdam.

in the real world, where the sheer power and strength of the 'what is' rules the day. We may wish for a different world but the reality is some way down the yellow brick road. So it's best to keep our heads down, live lives as close to the Jesus way as possible, build our churches, try to keep our children in faith and hopefully lead a few to Jesus and pray for a revival so a large number of people can come to church and we can go to heaven.

Sometimes this approach to faith reminds me of the Israelites who were rounded up, captured and marched off to Babylon to feed an empire. They sat and wept by the waters and remembered where they had come from; the false prophets told them to keep themselves to themselves, God was coming to set them free very soon, so 'don't unpack your luggage, keep pure, have as little engagement with the evil empire as you can get away with'. This was the day of small things, the moment to accept reality, create a gated ghetto community and wait for cavalry to come over the hill.

> This is what the LORD Almighty, the God of Israel, says to all those I carried into exile from Jerusalem to Babylon: 'Build houses and settle down; plant gardens and eat what they produce. Marry and have sons and daughters; find wives for your sons and give your daughters in marriage, so that they too may have sons and daughters. Increase in number there; do not decrease. Also, seek the peace and prosperity of the city to which I have carried you into exile. Pray to the LORD for it, because if it prospers, you too will prosper.'
> *Jeremiah 29:4-7*

However, then comes the word from the true prophet of God who says exactly the opposite: 'You want to run back, but I say stay exactly where you are. You want to rent and keep your options open, but I say buy and build houses. You want to live out of a suitcase; I say buy a wardrobe. You don't want to think long term; I say plant a garden that will take years to mature. You don't want to have kids in a foreign place, because they may stay there when you go home. I say have many children and make many babies and make sure your children have many babies. You say let's keep ourselves to ourselves, let's build a little bit of Jerusalem here, let's keep away from these unrighteous people as much as possible, let's hope they suffer and decrease and fall apart, but I say to you seek the peace and the prosperity of the city to which I have called you; this is your country now, they are your people, and if their lives flourish and prosper because you have embraced them you too will grow and increase.'

This is the vision that God wants us to get our heads around. We are to inhabit this world, to truly live in our streets, towns and cities, to bless these places with the Christian viruses of love, hope and joy. To see them flourish, change and reflect the glory of God, to see them expand, grow, improve, be transformed, to truly prosper in Christ. And as our land prospers and is transformed so too will we be transformed and grow and flourish. As we give we shall receive, as we bless we shall be blessed. This is the role of the Church in this big picture; the redemption of creation is to live like the kingdom that is coming, to be the primary means through which God brings in His renewed world.

Up until a few years ago I thought the gap between the bright dream and the dull reality was so wide that this was way beyond reach. However, the story contained within this book has radically changed that perception, because it unveils a hidden vista that God has been landscaping for years, a foundational work that creates the context for the dream to come into focus.

The major obstacle to imagining God's future is not the power of God to bring this about, or conceiving the biblical vision, but the position of the main means of grace to the world: the Church. We are the light on the hill where God displays His glory and the world looks on (Matthew 5:14). But herein lies the major problem – that light on the hill is not burning as brightly as it should.

We know that, of course, because we are all aware that the transformation needed in the world is first needed in us personally and corporately. Over these last few decades we have seen this growing transformation, with the renewal of our worship, our discipleship, our structures and our mission. Although the statistics still point to decline in the UK, a substantial section of the Church is better placed than it was. We now have healthier churches, with a better grasp on what they are about and what they are seeking to do. As the CEO of my council pointed out, we do have an impressive list of activities and service to the community: there is life, energy and vision.

However, we seriously lack a communal approach to mission. We each do our own thing in our own time, with our own resources, in our own patch. As individual denominations within dioceses or regional areas, there will be an attempt to get some joined-up activity, often with no reference to other denominations or independent churches. But what about a coordinated strategy? What about cooperation with other churches? What about a city-wide, transformative vision?

For significant transformation to happen in the villages, towns, boroughs and cities of our land, no individual church or denomination will be able to achieve much. However, together as one Church, living out the prayer of Jesus in John 17 to be one in spirit and purpose, we do have a foundation to work from. If Christ is drawing all things to Himself under His Lordship, He will be starting with His own body, the Church. If Christ has a vision for the transformation of 'all things', He will be starting from a base of His unified people who live the transformation vision of love, selflessness, forgiveness and healed relationships.

And this is exactly what Christ has been doing in our day all across the country for more than thirty years. Something very significant has been happening under the radar and hidden away: God has been doing a work behind the scenes in villages, towns and cities across the nation. This is not manufactured, copied, hyped or simply the latest fashionable thing to do. It is a work of the Spirit because it goes against the grain of human nature and challenges our need often to be independent, selfish and insular.

All over the county in villages, towns, boroughs and cities, church leaders, leaders of Christian agencies and Christian leaders in society are laying down their own agendas and differences to become friends, to pray together and work together for the sake of blessing the places they have been sent to serve. From Newcastle to Plymouth, from the north-east to the south-west, in more than 130 towns and cities, God has been building together an expression of Jesus' prayer in John 17:11, 21 'that they may be one ... so that the world may believe'.

From this platform of a growing unity, people are beginning to lift up their eyes towards a greater vision of praying and working for the transformation of their town or city, to believe that in two or three decades the place they live in could be substantially improved, culturally, socially and spiritually.

This isn't only a unity expressed among local churches and Christian charities, but also across the cultural spheres. Christians in business are beginning to connect and support each other, praying together for greater kingdom strategic alignment. Christians in the arts are forming close prayerful friendships across cities and towns, with a vision to see the cultural context blessed with *shalom*, resulting in more beautiful places, events, celebrations and exhibitions, reflecting the creator of the cosmos. Educationalists who love Christ and seek to bear faithful witness are creating contexts for support, inspiration and strategic action. This coming together of the Church in its widest sense is happening in media, sport, civic life, politics, family life and in other areas.

The dream for change in any place comes from a holy disquiet in the present context. My own place is our borough in Greater Manchester, called Trafford. Having served and lived in the area for more than thirty years, I know its great strengths and assets, but I also yearn for some fundamental change.

I love its context, connected at one end to central Manchester with its rich urban life, and at the other end to the beautiful Cheshire countryside. It was created during the 1970s reorganisation of local authorities, an amalgamation of five town councils. It struggles to have a central core identity that all can relate to, but it does have a wide variety of places and cultures, from the edgy, youthful and culturally diverse area of Old Trafford to the quant Cheshire countryside of Dunham, to the old money huge Victorian pies of Bowdon and the high-earning entrepreneurs of Hale, to the urban grittiness of Stretford and Partington.

In many ways it is a microcosm of the country, with urban areas, countryside, deprived neighbourhoods and very wealthy streets. It is the home to some significant national assets, such as God's favourite football team, Manchester United (!), and a few hundred yards away is Lancashire County Cricket Club. Both these clubs are situated close to Trafford Park, the largest business park in the UK, making Trafford the economic power house of the north-west of England, with the Trafford Centre, a huge shopping arena, providing a major guest venue.

I love this borough with its parks, its shops, its community life and its people. However, there is much I long to see changed.

I dream about a day when the gap between the very richest and poorest is reduced, a day when a poorer resident in a socially deprived area is able to live as long as the richer resident down the road and not die eleven years earlier, as now.

I dream about a day when the independent, self-centred culture in parts of the borough is replaced by a humble, civic-minded, interdependent culture.

I dream about a day when the five food banks in Trafford close down because people are being paid a living wage, and those out of work are supported to find employment quickly.

I dream about a day when there is no longer a 'them and us' culture between statutory authorities and citizens, a day when we all engage in a participative democracy, with the local needs and aspirations shaping the authorities' agendas.

I dream about a day when those most in need would be better served and cared for, the very poor, the sick, the depressed, the isolated, those with disabilities, those living in fear in homes and in the streets.

I dream about a day when there is a fairer education system in my borough that invests in the aspirations and talents of all its children.

I dream about marriages and partnerships to be lifelong loving relationships providing the basic emotional building blocks for our future generation.

I dream about a new level of communal living in streets all across the borough, where the elderly are supported, the lonely are befriended, and people feel good about knowing their neighbours and being part of the street.

I dream about a day when the churches are growing in size and depth of spirituality, a day when new churches are planted and more and more people are finding Christ.

A day when churches are so immersed in their communities that they are at the forefront of community life, partnering with authorities and other churches to provide and serve the place God has called them to bless.

I think transformation may look a bit like this.

As a pastor of a local church in Old Trafford, or a nurse at Trafford General Hospital, or a retired teacher, I may not be able to influence national government policy on benefits, financial cuts or foreign policy, but I can pray for my borough, I can be a great neighbour, I can try to influence some small decision in my place of work that makes for a better working environment, or results in a better service to the customer. I can love and be patient and pray for wisdom, I can meet with other pastors to pray and coordinate activity, I can form a small praying network of Christians in my hospital, I can believe that over time God will establish His kingdom a bit more each year. I can dream and work towards this vision of a new earth in my street, in my town, in my borough, in my city.

This book is the story of this move of God, to capture its vitality, scope and vision, to help inspire us all towards the transformation of the places God has called us to. This is a fresh missional perspective that challenges denominational thinking, selfish empire-building and small-minded parochial approaches.

Chapter 2
The Unveiling

In 2010, after twenty-two years in pastoral ministry at Altrincham Baptist Church I was undertaking a much-needed sabbatical, wondering where God was leading me in the future. I felt a rightness about staying in the Manchester area, and helping others shape and build a growing relational unity across the region. It was at this time that I got a call from Steve Clifford, who had recently been appointed as general director of the Evangelical Alliance. He sensed in his travels that God was doing a new thing in unity across towns and cities, and asked if I would be willing to go and find out what was happening. This began a wonderful journey of discovery that led to visiting many towns and cities across the nation and then around the world as God began to unveil what He had been doing for many years.

Like many others, I had some idea of what was happening at a national level with denominations and Christian organisations, and I had some knowledge of exemplary churches on the ground, but little understanding of God's missional work in other places.

As I got in my car, this narrow and limited perspective was about to end. Here are some brief examples of what I found in towns and cities in the UK and abroad.

York

'This had better be a good prayer meeting,' I muttered as my alarm clock rang at some unearthly hour. Getting from Manchester to York for a time of prayer at 7.30am is no small feat of commitment. I arrived in good time to be greeted by a rather gruff northern Pentecostal pastor, and shown into the predictable wooden-floored church hall to attend a prayer meeting of some pastors in York who belong to an organisation called One Voice York.

There had obviously been a meeting the previous evening because about forty-five chairs were still out, arranged in a circle. I began to do what every pastor in England does before an early-morning prayer meeting: I began to put away most of the chairs and rearrange a much smaller circle to make the room not feel too cavernous.

'What are you up to?' I was asked. 'Leave them as they are!' said my host.

I began to do as I was told and tell myself that the atmosphere wasn't my responsibility; obviously in York they don't mind about this sort of thing!

Then one by one people came into the room, slowly but surely filling every chair, and then they had to put more chairs out to accommodate the pastors who were arriving. I was shocked to be in such a well-attended and vibrant prayer meeting with more than fifty people present, all praying for God's blessing on the city of York. This, however, wasn't a one-off event, but a weekly occurrence, and had been going on since 1999!

This is no top-down bureaucratic organisation. One Voice has no membership, just a handful of trustees, but is a large network of Church leaders and leaders of associated ministries, across the denominations and traditions covering about 75 per cent of the churches and organisations in York. One Voice's life is rooted in this weekly Wednesday morning prayer meeting, after which they remain for tea and toast and relate as friends across traditions and streams and theologies. They operate in a spirit which is rooted in agreement and relationship rather than tradition or compromise. From this prayerful relational strength they have organised countless missions, celebrations and events. Over twenty charities and numerous ministries have been formed out of the foundation of unity across the city, including food banks, Street Angels, youth leaders' forums, community cafés, chaplaincies, a house of prayer and much more.

One of the most impressive mission events and examples of unified witness is the annual open-air baptism service conducted outside York Cathedral with Archbishop John Sentamu and leaders of other churches attracting hundreds of people. This is a vivid picture of what the Church can look like when it's joined together as one body in relationship and prayer for the sake of the city.

Chester: Link Up

Andy and Sue Glover, local church leaders and the main leaders of the unity for transformation movement in

Chester called Link Up, found themselves in a crisis, with Sue being diagnosed with MS. Their world changed overnight, with major concerns, confusion and anxiety. At times like these, you need your friends. The first group to come around and pray for them, to show love and concern, was the leadership group, Link Up Chester. Leaders from a variety of churches across the city gathered to stand with them and seek God for this shocked couple.

The unity that God has been growing in many different places across the country has at its core a relational, friendship-based approach that not only gives support and encouragement for leaders in times of need, but also provides an overall supportive atmosphere in which leaders can flourish.

Link Up, which now covers Chester and the wider Cheshire area, has, as one of its main strengths, the building of strong friendships among leaders, who, like One Voice York, regularly pray together but also go on retreat every year. There is a strong bond of mutual support that creates the foundation from which extensive cooperative mission can take place. Not only are the church leaders networked, but also the youth leaders and children's workers.

This strong relational emphasis has now spilled over towards the local authority, where increasing links between Link Up and Cheshire West and Chester Council have produced a faith audit survey that tracked the extensive work being carried out by faith groups across the region. This in turn has led to the appointment of a link worker whose role is to create greater connectivity between the faith group and the statutory authorities, paid for by the local authority.

Croydon: Croydon Churches Forum

The smell of smoke was heavy in the air as they gathered in the church hall, a group of more than 100 residents and shopkeepers who had had their lives turned upside down over the last twenty-four hours. The riots in the summer of 2011 had affected the area significantly, with cars burnt out and shops looted, people injured, with one fatality, and a large department store burnt to the ground. There was shock and fear and some anger at the apparent inability of the police to control society. The police needed to hold a public meeting to begin to communicate with the local people, but were concerned about the possible reaction, and contacted the Croydon Churches Forum (CCF) and asked if they would host and lead the meeting, which they agreed to do; they helped serve the community in the aftermath of this disaster.

The background to this strategic involvement by the churches was the fruit of years of prayer, unified witness and established friendships. This is an example of what can happen when churches get their act together, creating a unified way of relating and working with a vision to see the transformation of the places God has called them to live in.

CCF has been in existence for many years and grew out of the 'Churches Together' work across the city. Wanting a lighter touch, a more relational way of working, they formed the forum which exists to network the churches and work together in mission. It involves many churches and organisations across the city and presents the Church as one of the most active and important community structures. It has an impressive list of many activities and ministries they work on together, including the twenty-seven schools they run, and the thirty churches involved in providing a regular night shelter for homeless people across the city. They run a very successful town chaplaincy service alongside Street Pastors and school pastors and much more besides.

Stoke

When Stoke was declared the worst place to live in the country, church leaders and other Christians came together to pray for the town. What they didn't do was blame the council, the government or the economic circumstances. What they did do was to say, 'On our watch that happened!' They took spiritual responsibility for the place God had put them in; they knew instinctively that if they were a better expression of God's kingdom, more committed, prayerful, unified, integrated and missional, then the town might not be in the position it found itself in.

So they turned to prayer and a move of God's Spirit began. Large prayer meetings were followed up with conversations with civic leaders about the challenges ahead. This led initially to prayer for the renewal of the Church, and for improvement in high unemployment levels, the large numbers of young people not in education or training, and the recession. The main prayer request that continually came to the fore was that Stoke City would make the Premiership so that the morale in the city could be improved.

Over the last few years significant improvements have been seen across the city.

Unemployment has reduced, fewer children are outside the education and training systems, businesses are stronger than they were, and Stoke City FC gained entry to the Premier League. The Churches have grown and people have come to faith, and a major prayer house has been established.

Liverpool: Together for the Harvest

Together for the Harvest (TFH) was founded in 1998 when leaders from a group of churches were impressed with the importance of having strong, uniting relationships. Together those churches explored issues of purpose and vision, and began to dream of what would be possible when there was a unity in spirit with a strong focus on a common purpose: to see a harvest of people turning to the Lord Jesus in the Mersey region, and society changed by the adoption of biblical values in the spheres of influence in which they moved.

On the foundations of prayer, purpose and unity, TFH organised a number of region-wide evangelistic initiatives, including just10 with the evangelist J.John, held weekly for ten nights in the Anglican cathedral – more than 2,000 people came each week, many of whom were visitors; Merseyfest, a major coming together of more than 200 churches, and local community groups, with the police and other secular bodies. Two hundred social action projects were run in a week in summer 2005, culminating in a two-day festival, free to enter, for the public. Official estimates said that 75,000 people came over the two days in Croxteth Park.

Plymouth Churches Together

The Plymouth unity movement is unusual in today's vibrant unity world, since it is a resurrected Churches Together organisation. Plymouth is a vibrant, growing strategic movement led by Chris Clewer, a local church leader. Over the last three years, he and a number of others have managed to make the big jump from institution to movement.

They look and sound very similar to other movements I have visited, with a mixture of leaders' gatherings, a good website, prayer focus and day conferences, being a hub of communication for the Church and organisations in the city.

They also have a growing vision for transformation of the whole city, and have completed a very successful faith audit survey. Interestingly, they shaped the survey around the structure of the Local Strategic Partnership for Plymouth so that it could communicate the great work the faith groups do in society.

Tyneside: Together in Christ Tyneside

Together in Christ draws together more than forty leaders from the charismatic, Pentecostal and evangelical wings of the Church. They meet to pray every week and have regular leaders' teaching days in a 4-star hotel on the waterfront. The movement has birthed Street Pastors and Healing on the Streets across the city. Both are shining examples of the ministries, and J.John came recently and held a large mission there. Eden has also opened, with four centres already set up. There is a strong bond of love and affirmation among the leaders of the churches, and they have much to teach others about the values of honouring each other in Christ.

Southampton: Love Southampton

Love Southampton provides a strong relational base and a common mission strategy following Hope 08. There is a growing church planting strategy developing, looking to see vibrant churches in every neighbourhood. The network does successfully manage to bring together a wide variety of evangelical expressions, from the Pentecostal to the more conservative wing.

Once a term they gather leaders to a big lunch with a speaker, and once a year about forty leaders go on a retreat. They see the keys to developing this sort of network as being:

1. Father and mother figures who have served long-term in the city;

2. Development of good friendships;

3. Emphasis on kingdom not empire-building;

4. Prayer.

When New Community Church went through serious problems, a number of leaders in the city stood with them. This practical support at a time of need has deepened relationships and trust.

The network is developing a vision for the whole city, and not just personal and Church renewal. Links are developing with the city council and the health authorities.

The most exciting development is the challenge to find at least forty fostering and adoptive families for the city. So far they have managed to find more than eighty families. This has brought a new-found respect within the council, and has opened up other opportunities.

Reading: Reading Christian Network

2017 is the twentieth anniversary of this network. They have prayed together every week and worked alongside each other to develop numerous social action charities, evangelistic initiatives and cultural sphere engagements. They have an effective strategic partnership with the local civic authorities and are becoming a valued service provider to the town. It is no surprise that The Turning, a major evangelistic ministry, started in Reading and has now spread all over the country.

All over the world

This surprising movement of unity for the transformation of cities and towns is not only found in this country but all across the world. I was privileged to attend one of the very first Movement Days in New York where the New York

City Leadership Center, supported by Tim Keller, the pastor of the Redeemer Presbyterian Church, began to invite people who have a similar vision. I met there with city leaders from all over the world who had the same values and vision as the unity movements we discovered in the UK.

It was exciting to hear about the churches coming together in Portland, USA, to serve the city council. It was wonderful to hear about the unity across the town of Toowoomba in Australia where church leaders had been praying and working together for many years, producing significant joined-up mission activities alongside exciting social action projects. It was a joy to meet the leaders from Together for Berlin who had been linking churches and Christian charities for more than twenty years. For a city not known for its unity-building during the twentieth century, a humble, gentle movement of unity had grown up, not seeking to rule over the city, but to serve and bless all that God was doing. It was staggering to hear about 1,200 churches working as one body across Mumbai, called Mumbai Christian Network, in one of the largest cities in the world with a population of more than twenty million. From Africa to New Zealand, from South America to Europe, God is on the move, building His body, creating a context and platform for His grace to effect kingdom transformation.

After unearthing this significant move of God, in conversation with many of the leaders of these unity movements it was felt there was a need to form a relational network that would begin to unite the cities and towns in order to share best practice and support each other. There was also a need to look at where unity for mission wasn't happening, and to encourage it to begin and to raise awareness of this missional perspective across the Church in the UK. The Evangelical Alliance led by Steve Clifford was extremely supportive of this initiative and provided the majority of funding to get it off the ground, explaining that they wanted to simply support and cheer on this move of God without any control or ownership. That gracious and servant-hearted approach enabled Gather to be born. Gather was founded in 2011 as a relational network of these vibrant unity movements across the nation. It now has more than 130 city and town movements as part of its network and is the driving force behind Movement Day UK.

Where has the influence of these movements come from?

The extraordinary aspect of this fresh move of unity is that there seems to be no one source of influence. There is no famous church driving the interest, there is no one well-known city to visit to get your unity vision from. This is also not the latest fashion on the Christian scene, as it's been going for more than thirty years. This is, I believe, a move of the Holy Spirit that has been building and growing for years, arising from many different sources of inspiration and theological perspective. There is a gathering momentum that is building across the world that will one day become the norm for all churches and Christians in cities and towns.

This gathering momentum is being fuelled from numerous sources that together are creating a fast-flowing river of mission. Here are some of the main influencing sources, both historic and contemporary, across the UK and the world at the present time.

1.   Ecumenical movement

The seeds of this movement of unity are found in the modern ecumenical movement which began at the beginning of the twentieth century and gained momentum following the devastation of the Second World War. This was expressed in church life, with the formation of the World Council of Churches in 1948 which was superseded in the UK in 1990 by the Churches Together in Britain and Ireland.

While this form of unity was seen by some as lacking the relational and, at times, strong missional thrust, it was the deep desire of many that the body of Christ could be and should be more united. The development of more relational and missional unity movements across the UK as detailed in this book owe in part their foundations to the work of the wider ecumenical movement over the twentieth century. It has been very encouraging in particular to see the work of Churches Together in England firstly giving freedom and encouragement to Churches Together groups across cities and towns to explore a more relational and missional expression of unity, and also supporting the newer Gather-type unity movements that are arising. Gather has very close links to Churches Together in England and the two are very supportive of each other.

2. Charismatic influence

One of the hallmarks of the early charismatic movement was its expression of unity across denominational divides. The movement was at grass roots level and brought together Anglicans with Catholics, Baptists and Pentecostals – even the Brethren were meeting with Methodists.

Kevin Ranaghan regards this unity as 'the largest grassroots ecumenical movement that Christianity has known for 450 years'.[3]

The World Council of Churches in 1975 also regard the charismatic renewal as 'a major ecumenical development of our day' and they identify their responsibility to 'discern grass-roots ecumenical development of worldwide significance'.[4]

Personally having come to faith in Christ at the age of fifteen in the mid 1970s through the witness of a charismatic youth group based in an Anglican church, I assumed all Christians linked across denominations. I vividly remember singing 'Bind Us Together', attending the musical called *Come Together* and being part of larger charismatic gatherings that attracted congregations and speakers from across many denominations. The leading lights of the movement came from the Church of England

---

[3] Quoted in Tom Smail, 'Editorial: The More We Are Together …', *Renewal*, No 71 (October–November 1977), p2.

[4] World Council of Churches, 'A Statement of Concerns (1975)', in Kilian McDonnell (ed) *Presence, Power, Praise: Documents on the Charismatic Renewal*, Vol III: International Documents, Numbers 1-11, 1973-1980 (Collegeville, MN: Liturgical Press, 1980), p283.

(David Watson, Colin Urquhart, Michael Harper), Baptists (David Pawson) and Catholics (Francis MacNutt).

In more recent years, leaders from within the Pentecostal and charismatic movements, such as Ed Silvoso, and others across the world have approached the call for unity for mission from a city-wide transformational agenda. Building on the call and experience of unity within the charismatic tradition, they extended this to include a missional agenda to see the transformation of whole cities and towns. Silvoso, as the most prominent of these leaders, focused on Church unity as a prerequisite for transformation, with a strategy to enable Christians in the marketplace and a goal to reduce systemic poverty. A number of Gather-type unity movements owe their existence to the teaching and encouragement of Silvos's ministry and others.

3. Reformed influence

Tim Keller in New York, and others, have been working from the Reformed perspective, developing what is called a 'Gospel Movement'. Inspired by their Calvinistic heritage, they consider transformation to be taking place when the Christian population is growing faster than the general population in a city/region. They are also looking for local churches to reach new people with the gospel and for transformation of the lives of young people, the poor and marginalised. They are seeking to encourage Christians in the cultural spheres to exercise their faith and influence in every sector of society and for city-wide networks to grow up that mobilise, develop and connect these leaders.

Keller believes that when all of these elements work together to make the gospel of grace, truth, mercy and justice visible and tangible, then the kingdom of God will become more real in the life of each city.

4. Prayer movements

Over the last thirty or so years, a groundwork of intercessory prayer has been undertaken by individuals, groups and organisations for towns and cities. This is now being developed further with the advent of Houses of Prayer, the 24–7 prayer movement and the World Prayer Centre in Birmingham. Connecting with more than 130 unity movements in towns and cities across the nation, I've not yet found a story of developing unity for mission that has not been grounded and supported by people who simply prayed for the places God has called them to serve.

5. HOPE 08/14 influence

A number of Gather-type unity movements owe their formation to the Hope 08 initiate for mission across the UK. With its focus on reaching villages, towns and cities by doing more mission together, it kick-started some key cities in their long-term expression of unity for mission as a growing expression of Church in the UK.

6. Whole-life discipleship influence

The work of the London Institute of Contemporary Christianity and of the Jubilee Centre has done much to highlight the need for Christians in the workplace to show and declare Christ in all sectors of life. While not strictly having a town and city transformational agenda, it does feed into the vision by urging churches to train and release their members to be kingdom influencers in the cultural and social spheres of society.

7. Movement Day

Begun in 2010, Movement Day is a one- to three-day catalytic event to bring together the stories and experience of Christians from different churches and spheres of society. Using the terminology of developing Gospel Movements, they focus on finding solutions to the 'stubborn facts' plaguing cities such as crime, poverty, apathy, failed educational systems, unemployment, etc. Their approach is to multiply the impact of one – through the unity of many. Global Cities Movement Day was held in October 2016 in New York, attracting more than 3,000 participants from more than ninety-five nations, and plans are being made to extend this event to other cities around the world.

The essential dynamics of these unity movements

My own experience of unity, working across a local area for much of my ministry in the south Manchester area, was very hit and miss. It mainly fell into two categories: firstly, the local ecumenical structure, with a ministers' fraternal with its three-monthly soup-and-bread lunchtime meeting that at the very least got us to meet each other, but was characterised by stilted conversation and uncomfortable silences.

Added to this were three-monthly committee meetings, often not attended by ministers, and a week of prayer for Christian unity. My own personal experience of this form of unity was disappointing, with its lack of close relationships and a missional focus.

There were times when the local churches responded with some enthusiasm to a missional initiative. A committee was formed, actions were planned and the event was held, often successfully. However, this activity, on top of the heavy demands of pastoral ministry, often meant most church leaders breathed a sigh of relief when the event was over and they went back to normal life soon afterwards. Usually, a new pastor arrived in the area and had a great idea for some joint working, and the cycle of planning, delivering and retreating began again. This had some merit, but it certainly was not a coordinated strategic approach to seeing the area transformed.

Most church leaders of all varieties when faced with this experience of ecumenicalism have disengaged from the process, rightly concluding that it's a better use of time and resources to get on with doing your own thing in your own church. But this all too common approach is a parody of what unity is meant to be and is a million miles away from the energy, focus and effectiveness of these networks forming all over the country. What makes them so different? Why are they being sustained over many years? What gives them the dynamism that more traditional approaches have found lacking?

Three core foundational dynamics

Relational

As we have already stated, these movements are fuelled by a strong relational dynamic alongside a sustained commitment to prayer for the area they have been called to serve. People gather regularly, often over many years, not because they have to, but because they want to. This is no top-down command from the denominational HQ to attend, but a personal commitment because they have formed long-lasting friendships over a period of time with people they trust and enjoy being with and praying alongside.

Many church leaders can find themselves isolated and lonely, around people all day long with many demands on their resources, but at the same also without friends and emotional support, giving out but often not receiving.

One pastor who attended a weekly unity for transformation meeting in his city said that he viewed the week starting on a Wednesday when the leaders met for prayer, because he felt he was part of a wider team called to reach the city. He was able to talk about his joys and fears, challenges and successes, in a safe supportive context.

The power of friendship is a much undervalued aspect of the kingdom of God. Jesus calls us to be His friends, we are called into a community of mutual supportive friendship, as it says in Proverbs: 'A friend loves at all times, and a brother [or sister] is born for a time of adversity' (17:17). Ministry is hard enough in this secular, consumerist society; we need to learn what it is to stand with each other, supporting each other towards the greater goal of the transformation of society.

These unity movements are creating firesides for people to gather around. Some leaders won't see the need as much as others, some have ministry teams they are part of, but most deeply value the commitment that brothers and sisters in ministry can make to one another.

The Bible also takes this deeper friendship-based unity to another level when it says that this commitment we make in relationships to one another is in itself a witness to the world, a deep truth of the kingdom that will in turn result in the world knowing more about God (see John 13:34; 15:17). The command to love one another is not an added extra to the Christian journey; it is at the core of the Faith, and that command cannot just be narrowed to those from my church or my denomination, it surely must extend to those in Christ across the whole spectrum of traditions and expressions.

Living in a highly individualistic Western world – where people and groups often exist in isolation from others, operating in their own agenda silos – is a huge challenge to the Church to live and operate differently, to grow a partnership culture instead of having a self-centred, inward-looking approach.

Prayerful

Alongside close relationships, prayer is at the very core of these unity movements. Regular sustained prayer is carried out over many years, often either weekly or monthly, with leaders from churches, Christian organisations and Christians in the ordinary spheres of life. The agenda is to bless the city, to pray for its needs and challenges, to pray for its spiritual, social and cultural revival. Town-wide missional initiatives will be interceded for, and often leaders pray for each other and the needs they have at that particular moment. Prayer is seen as a priority, not an added extra, with the needs of the city paramount in the focus.

Missional

They are all highly motivated to see their areas changed by the power of the gospel. These are missional movements that believe they can achieve much more together than apart, and want to share resources to enable the kingdom to come in their place. This is not ecumenicalism for its own sake, but real relational unity for the sake of mission. The mission is to see spiritual transformation, with people's lives being changed by meeting Christ, but also to see cultural and social transformation, where a town or city can be affected by the kingdom of God.

It is the interplay and trifold focus of all three dynamics that is creating the energy and enthusiasm of these unity movements.

- To be prayerful and missional without unity is disjointed.

- To be missional and unified without prayer is to be disempowered.

- To be prayerful and unified without mission is to be directionless.

Theologians can tend to disagree about which dynamic is primary, some arguing that the call to unity is most important, with others arguing that mission is the main focus and that the call to unity is one subset of the missional agenda, or that prayer is the fundamental foundation to all activity of the kingdom. However your theological priority list is composed, it is very clear that without all three components operating together, no real, sustained and enduring transformation can occur. All of God's people need to join in unity as the one body of Christ across a place, calling out in prayer to the Holy Spirit for Christ's glory to come as they go out to follow the missional God into their town or city.

Other dynamics …

Organised with good leadership and effective communication hubs

Most of the movements are started by an individual or a small group of leaders. These key community gatherers start by drawing a small group together, and from that base create a 'must join' movement. Strong, prayerful friendships are attractive to other leaders, who may be isolated and lonely.

The leadership structures are often very flat, with a few leaders playing the role of enablers; each movement does have recognised leaders who have been affirmed in that role. The leadership is very much servant-based and more pastoral in nature, but it does take respected and gifted people to lead leaders from across the denominational, organisational and other networks.

Linked to a purposeful leadership structure, these movements also have very effective communication hubs that span the work of many churches and organisations, and can be very effective tools for the kingdom. Most of these movements have good websites and effective social media communication, creating tremendous opportunities, where the individual churches are only able to provide one phone number and one leadership team for civic authorities to engage with.

Core values and theology

The movements on the whole all share some key values/cultures and theological insights that provide the real energy and sustainability for their work.

1.   A preferring of and respect for one another

When attending a unity for mission meeting, you are struck by the lack of posturing and egotism; while not perfect, they are, on the whole, places where there is a relaxed atmosphere, much humour and a humility of heart towards each other. A strong mutual respect exists, focusing on developing a culture where everyone is welcome, respected and affirmed. Bible verses such as 'make my joy complete by being like-minded, having the same love, being one in spirit and of one mind … value others above yourselves' (Philippians 2:2-3) help create a loving and deferential culture.

2.   Culture of informality and flat leadership structures

These unity movements have very little bureaucracy, with no minutes of meetings taken and votes to make decisions; they are very informal with flat leadership structures. However, do not conclude that relational informality creates disorganisation and ineffectiveness; these are well-organised movements with enough structure to help support the life of the movement, with decisions being made after consultation, and much conversation. Because of the relational closeness and a commitment to certain values, decisions are often made quickly and effectively.

3. Diversity within unity

While there are significant theological, cultural, ecclesiastical and practical differences between churches in any city or town, these could potentially be major barriers to relating and working together within Gather-type movements. In fact, the opposite is the case – the differences are seen as a benefit because there is a high value placed on the celebration of diversity. This is a far cry from the lowest common denominator approach of some ecumenicalism, where the fear of causing offence produces a bland, colourless approach. From the perspective of diversity, we celebrate the differences and we learn from each other's traditions and cultures. Unity within diversity celebrates the African Church, who teach us about the value of joy, giving, and the importance of fasting. The Methodists challenge us to value social justice, the Pentecostals urge us to focus on the Holy Spirit, and the Anglicans show us how to relate to the state and its civic structure. The Catholics help root us theologically through the centuries, and the evangelicals urge us to hold to the centrality of the Bible, conversion through the cross, and activism. Over the last few years, we've had the privilege of worshipping within many different contexts, and we always ask ourselves the question: what can I learn from this tradition – where do I see Jesus within this context?

4. Emphasising the essentials of the faith to unify them theologically

From a foundation of celebrating diversity within unity comes a respect for each other's theological differences. A new mature form of unity is emerging, where people can have significant differences on many themes but still choose to stay and work together, respecting each other's differences but agreeing to disagree in grace about non-essentials. Unity theologically is being built around the Apostles' Creed and the centrality of Christ for the sake of mission to the city or town. Gather-type unity movements don't always do all things together – certain events, conferences and activities can sometimes suit certain groupings of churches – but often they are able to work together on major social projects and mission events, such as a joint Alpha course. The basis of their unity is the constant relational friendship and sustained prayer.

5. A belief that kingdom matters more than empire-building

This is an underlying value and essential to the transformational agenda that Christians are, at the end of the day, not driven by ego, power and prominence, but by a love for their city or town and a self-sacrificing attitude that seeks to build the kingdom, regardless of position and recognition. What matters is that the city is served and Christ is glorified.

6. The garden prayer

Unity movements are motivated not only by the desire for closer friendships and the importance of better strategic and coordinated action, but, more importantly, by the biblical call for unity expressed by Christ. The Old Testament, with its constant emphasis on love of neighbour and the formation of the people of God, is taken to its high point in the New Testament into the 'gathering in and unifying' of all things under Christ:

> he made known to us the mystery of his will according to his good pleasure, which he purposed in Christ, to be put into effect when the times reach their fulfilment – to bring unity to all things in heaven and on earth under Christ.
> *Ephesians 1:9-10*

This overall thread of theology is crystallised in the call from the garden:

> My prayer is not for them alone. I pray for those who will believe in me through their message, that all of them may be one, Father, just as you are in me and I am in you. May they also be in us so that the world may believe that you have sent me … I in them and you in me – so that they may be brought to complete unity. Then the world will know you sent me and have loved them even as you have loved me.
> *John 17:20-23*

We must work together in unity because it is the very nature of God as three-in-one, a mutual coexistence of love and affirmation overflowing to creation and humanity. We are drawn into this Trinitarian relationship as brothers and sisters adopted in the family; we are the body of Christ on earth, living as the new humanity in relational forgiving unity, becoming a light on the hill to the world.

Unity is not an added extra of the gospel, it is not a nice thing to do sometimes and then be dropped for something more important; it is not a new missional strategy that could be changed if necessary, depending on the context. Unity is core to our faith and practice, and without it we are forever weakened and inauthentic. Without it we bring our faith in God into disrepute and embarrassment.

City- and town-wide gifting emerge

It's interesting in our ever-developing individualistic world that Scripture is read through that isolation lens. When approaching passages such as Ephesians 4:11, where Paul lists some of the main gifting within the body, these are usually interpreted either across a singular denomination or across a local church. So apostles, prophets, evangelists, pastors and teachers become the sole preserve of an individual theological persuasion or a single local church. However, the letter to the Ephesians was written to a city-wide church, probably with some different expressions of faith within the house church/extended family context, and the giftings listed are overlaid across that paradigm. People are then recognised not just within the local house church context of the early Church, but across the whole city. Prophets began to minster widely, teachers must have moved from house church to house church, and evangelists operated across the area.

When the unified body of Christ emerges in a town or city in contemporary unity movements, the gifts of the Spirit are increasingly recognised across many denominations. Within these groups, some key leaders emerge with gifts that bless the wider body. People with prophetic, apostolic, pastoral, teaching gifts, etc, begin to express that gifting across a number of churches in an area. Alongside this individual gifting, whole-Church gifting is also expressed, with places recognising that some churches have particular callings that bless the wider body.

Here in Greater Manchester, we are increasingly recognising the evangelic ministry of Andy Hawthorne and the Message Trust, and particular churches and other individuals; we honour and welcome the teaching ministry of colleges and some key churches, the prophetic gifting of individuals and ministries, and the apostolic gifting in a number of key leaders in the region, both across local churches and other spheres of life. This perspective then begins to fuel imagination and faith to believe that together with the gifts of the Holy Spirit, we may begin to believe that our places could look different in years to come.

Developing sense of place and belonging

One interesting observation about this growing phenomenon is the increased commitment to geographical areas. With the dominance of postmodernity and the onset of globalisation, we are increasingly becoming dislocated from our places; as Craig Bartholomew says, 'place has become something that one moves through, preferably at great speed and virtual reality is no replacement'.[5] There is, it seems, a cultural reaction to the world as our village, with a growing rise in nationalism, regionalism and an increasing identity shaped by the town we come from or the city we live in. I wonder if unity movements are mirroring this change on a local level? 'Where do I belong?' is a big question for many people and it's a question for leaders of churches and congregations. Does a national identity in a denomination really provide enough? Perhaps a love of my city or town can bind me closer to the others?

Places all have different histories with developed cultures, creating a pride and love of an area. I may define myself as part of a particular denomination or stream of theology, and I may be called to a particular ministry, but I am also defined by the place I came from and the place I live in. With the rise and growth of the new churches, one expression of their ministry is to stay longer in places than the more established denominations; this has created, I believe, the context for more coordination and strategic unity-based development. The longer a leader stays in a town or city, the more identified they may become with its culture, its assets and aspirations; from this closer identification with place can arise a missional perspective beyond the formation of a local church towards a vision to affect the whole town or city.

---

[5] Craig G Bartholomew, *Where Mortals Dwell: A Christian View of Place for Today* (Grand Rapids, MI: Baker Academic, 2011), p3.

More theological study is now being undertaken to read the Bible through the lens of place, to understand the story begins in a garden, is shaped by a dream for a promised land, and finds its fulfilment in a holy city called Jerusalem, ending in a final vision for a renewed perfected city in Revelation. Jesus was born in Bethlehem, lived in Nazareth, ministered in Galilee and died in Jerusalem. His followers were sent out to strategic cities of the day from Antioch to Corinth, from Ephesus to Philippi and eventually to the centre of the empire, Rome. It's hard to fully read the Bible unless you see the importance of place in the development of humanity through the gospel.

Brueggemann summarises this cultural shift that is driving city- and town-based unity.

> That promise concerned human persons who could lead detached, unrooted lives of endless choice and no commitment. It was glamorized around the virtues of mobility and anonymity that seems so full of promise for freedom and self-actualization. But it has failed ... It is now clear that a sense of place is a human hunger that urban promise has not met ... It is rootlessness and not meaninglessness that characterizes the current crisis. There are no meanings apart from roots.[6]

---

[6] Walter Brueggemann, *The Land; Place as Gift, Promise, and Challenge in Biblical Faith* (Philadelphia, PA: Fortress, 1977), pp3-4.

Vision for spiritual, cultural and social transformation

A number of the unity movements do have an increasing vision for the spiritual, cultural and social transformation of their areas. They are not content to only evangelise and see churches renewed; they also want to see change. They have a heart for justice and peace; they want people to be lifted out of poverty and for the area to prosper. This is the driving force behind our Victorian forebears, those who led the civic gospel movement in Birmingham, lifting it out of poverty in the mid nineteenth century; it was the impetus behind some of the great reformers, such as Wilberforce, the Cadbury family and Sir Titus Salt in Bradford.

Calling forth the true nature of the place/culture

A number of unity movements have begun to pray to seek God as to the true nature of their city. Places develop a personality of their own; they are constructs of history, environment, context, weather, geographical positioning, wealth or poverty and opportunities and challenges. This results in Newcastle having a very different personality to Guildford and Liverpool having a different attitude to life than Bath. Berlin and Nuremberg have the weight of Nazi history on their shoulders following the war, which deeply influences the present and the future, even generations afterwards. New York is deeply influenced by its financial centre, its immigration and, more recently, the atrocity of 9/11.

Cities operate more as organisms becoming more than the sum of their parts, creating health or unhealthy outcomes. Organisms are more than the addition of single cells they synergise to become something different. Cities are more than the sum of individuals in a place; they are the organic entities that seem to have a life force in themselves. London is a very different organism to New York: both are large internationals centres of commerce and culture with a shared language but they have different attitudes, approaches and character. They are different places, with different personalities, challenges, opportunities and aspirations.

The question then comes as to how God sees a city. How does God relate to this unique organism? What dreams does God have for its future? What is its true nature under Christ? Can a city or town have a future in God? Certainly God in the Bible spoke a future over Nineveh, Jerusalem, and even a blessing over Babylon. Can a city with a difficult past move on and become a place of opportunity?

Chapter 3
For the Love of One Another

Two are better than one,
because they have a good return for their labour:
if either of them falls down,
one can help the other up.
But pity anyone who falls
and has no one to help them up.
Also, if two lie down together, they will keep warm.
But how can one keep warm alone?
Though one may be overpowered,
two can defend themselves.
A cord of three strands is not quickly broken.
(*Ecclesiastes 4:9-12*)

Having visited many of the unity movements referred to in this book, I have always been struck by the easy, warm atmosphere when you enter a meeting. The bright laughter and the kind words all create a welcoming loving context for relationships to flourish. If you were a new pastor or leader of a Christian charity arriving in the town, you would feel immediately embraced and accepted; you would recognise a safe place where support and encouragement would be offered. Leaders join unity movements not because they have to, not because they are told to, but because they want to. These are very busy people with many demands on their time and energy; however, they regular carve out significant time to meet and pray together because they have become friends. It is the power of friendship that is driving this emerging phenomenon. As I mentioned earlier, one city leader said to me, 'Wednesday mornings at the unity early morning prayer meeting is where I begin my week. I meet with my team, feel encouraged and supported and go out to the work of ministry. If it was not for this unity movement I would not have survived in ministry.'

One of the more relationally stronger movements is Link Up in Chester. Baptist minister Andy Glover speaks from many years of experience leading the Link Up network from across Chester and West Cheshire where on top of their regular meetings they hold annual leaders' retreats. Each autumn, for the past fifteen years, leaders and senior leadership teams from the churches across Chester take two to three days out of their busy schedules for valuable time away to pray, talk, eat and reflect. Around forty church leaders gather, catching the vision to give time to collective reflection, prayer and relationship-building in a beautiful quiet space. They have also formed small prayer support groups that meet weekly, in which leaders can share life and become accountable to one another; these aren't only for church leaders but also support networks for employed youth workers, student workers and, more recently, business leaders. Andy Glover says:

For we believe that through relationship and partnership we can see the Kingdom of God advance throughout our city, region, nation and world. At Link Up, we believe in partnership without ownership.

Meaningful relationships provide strength, support and accountability. 'If iron sharpens iron', to be effective in our God-given calling and our local mission we need accountable relationships in which others help, encourage and challenge us along the way.

For me there are at least ten reasons why we need meaningful relationship as church leaders with other church leaders from other churches in our city or town:

- Meaningful relationships demonstrate the unity in the body of Christ (John 17:20-23).

- Meaningful relationships reduce a spirit of competition and encourage a spirit of sharing (1 Corinthians 1:12-13; Colossians 4:16).

- Meaningful relationships encourage accountability to those who share the same vision and understand the constraints (Luke 19:12-27).

- Meaningful relationships encourage humility in larger churches and organisations as they acknowledge that they do not have all the answers, but can learn from others (1 Corinthians 4:6-7, 18).

- Meaningful relationships help smaller churches and organisations to feel they are making a contribution beyond their own limited resources (1 Corinthians 12:21-25).

- Meaningful relationships recognise that we live in a complicated world and that only by working together and sharing our combined, God-given wisdom and resources, will we accomplish the task (Ecclesiastes 4:9-12).

- Meaningful relationships allow us to brainstorm together, share varying approaches, evaluate different strategies, learn from the mistakes and successes of others and provide some benchmarking for future activity (Proverbs 13:10).

- Meaningful relationships often encourage greater stewardship and efficiency by joining together to share facilities, reducing duplication and limiting waste. It can lead to considerations of merger (Titus 3:14).

- Meaningful relationships help support and lift up those who are struggling in the task (Isaiah 35:1-4).

- Meaningful relationships free us to rejoice in success from wherever it originates (Philippians 1:12-14).

Over the last four years, Watford have also held a residential 'retreat' in the New Year and these have been powerful times of sharing, eating, praying and dreaming together. I was privileged to join them for their retreat in 2016. This year, 2017, they had thirty-seven leaders together for two days and Tim Roberts, one of the leaders, comments:

> The most inspiring stories include those friendships that have grown across denominational divides, between Protestant and Roman Catholic, and across generations too, with youth leaders and senior ministers sharing stories and meals together. We have now developed this further through the establishing of 'Unity Groups' – there are currently ten in operation – prayer triplets that meet as frequently as once a week in some cases, for mutual support and encouragement.

Tim Roberts is lead minister at Wellspring Church in Watford, just north of London, and part of the leadership team of Christians Across Watford. He remembers one of their earliest meetings in 1999 where they held a foot-washing ceremony:

> This was a profound pride-shattering, relationship-bonding moment and has been repeated on a couple of occasions since. It is absolutely essential to explore ways to bring dignity in a locality to churches and leaders irrespective of their size, other growth, 'success' indicators.

The simple act of the washing of feet places everyone on an equal footing (it emphasises our shared humanity); there is a vulnerability and a gentleness at work through this ritual that we should practise more often in our times together. To perform a physical act like this is often more meaningful and humbling, speaking to our haptic, bodily memory more than just the spoken word, and uniting us as one body, not just through our minds and our shared ideas, but also through our intimate and material selves. Tim Roberts says:

We need to be much better at celebrating each other's successes and testifying to what God is doing through different churches and ministries. We need to involve more diverse leaders in small-group accountability and prayerful, prophetic encouragement.

Ian Mayer, a businessman from Doncaster, also leads One Heart One Voice. He is passionate about unity going further than just among church leaders and has spent the past ten years growing relationships with both church and business leaders to influence their town. Ian has also worked with me in developing the Gather Network and has been a part of our team for many of our Gather conferences and workshops. He says:

I love the mathematical definition of unity, 'a quantity assuming the value of one'. There is a sense here of defining 'quantity' in the singular, rather than in the plural. Imagine the Church across a locality choosing to be identified in the singular rather than the plural. Every denomination, every stream and flavour saying, we choose to be known as one. What would such a Church look like? Are we brave enough to walk a path like this? Is it even a choice?

Years of research by different members of our family has shown that our family is made of hundreds of parts, and scattered across many locations. Each element is different to the other, and no unit is identical or uniform. Each has their own identity and each stands alone. However, we all consider ourselves part of one family because we are all united under one name, 'Mayer'. It's interesting as we have discovered the diversity and stumbled across new branches; our family has grown in size but still remains one. Sometimes when we are trying to unpack the meaning of something it is more helpful to describe what it is not. Unity is not uniformity or conformity. It's not about creating a structure that contains, restricts or controls. It's not even coming to a combined agreement on particular difficult issues. Unity is simply a relationship. It's a way of standing with others, despite differences in substance and style, and saying 'we are one'. We reside under one name, the name of Jesus.

It's clear from the Scripture that oneness with each other *and Christ are not optional.* Being 'as one' is the desire of Christ. In separating, dividing and disputing, we throw doubts upon the oneness of the Christian Faith and we take glory away from Christ. The world will not be persuaded by doctrine or good argument. It will not yearn for communion with the Father on the basis of well-argued theology. It will not turn from destruction to hope because of moral judgements and condemnation. The world will yearn for the Father, when it sees a Church that is one with itself and one with Christ.

Unity is most definitely relational, it is prayerful and it is missional. It's not just about doing things together, and it's certainly not polite ecumenicalism. Although ecumenical movements and initiatives can be great foundations for unity movements, they are not the relational unity we are referring to here. I'm defining unity here quite distinctively. Unity is rooted in Jesus' words in John 17. It's an attitude of heart that in being relational spills out across a locality. It impacts those who are involved in it and who join the journey, but more than that, it infects those around it. It changes communities and it feeds a growing Christian presence as it permeates localities. Unity should exist in ourselves as leaders and with the group we lead.

Back in the late 1990s something extremely powerful happened in Doncaster, south Yorkshire. A small group of church ministers met together and committed themselves to pray regularly for each other and the town. The group wasn't the idea of a single person and it wasn't formed by a committee. It was sparked by a move of the Holy Spirit that touched the hearts of a few church leaders. Initially the group consisted of just eight ministers from eight denominations, but today that group forms the core of a strategic network of many, many churches across the borough of Doncaster.

Admittedly there has been some formality added to the group over the years, and now under the banner of Mission Doncaster (and One Heart One Voice), this group continues to help local churches develop closer relationships, joined-up thinking, and a shared vision for the town. Even with this added formality, the key point is that this group is still relational. It's not based on structure but on sacrifice and service. This group does not consider itself 'the church in the city', or a super-community of some kind, under apostles. It's a group that acknowledges the complementary roles we have in our joint call to see God's kingdom come. There is a voluntary recognition and acceptance of each other as part of the wider body of Christ.

Another church leader who is motivated by a desire to work and partner with others rather than establish his own patch is Nic Harding. For many years he was founding pastor at Frontline Church in Liverpool, which he planted in 1991. Here he formed strong relationships with other pastors in the city and was part of the original formation of Together for the Harvest, a network of Christian leaders and a family of churches from across the Liverpool city region. After nearly thirty years, Nic is still one of its leaders, promoting their values of:

1. Connecting – helping like-minded leaders and churches connect with each other for encouragement and mutual cooperation;

2. Championing – recognising what God is doing in different parts of the region and celebrating those breakthroughs;

3. Communicating – so that all can know what churches and organisations across the region are doing, and what opportunities are arising;

4. Catalysing – naming and sharing a vision that others want to buy into, for the sake of the gospel in our region;

5. Coordinating – linking networks and organising events and activities, where this serves the purpose of our shared mission.

He writes:

> I am motivated to work for unity because I believe it will take the whole church to reach the whole region. I believe that we are 'Better Together' as the previous Anglican Bishop and Catholic Archbishop of Liverpool wrote. I believe our denominations are an aberration from the biblical norm of 'the Church in the house, and the Church in the city'. We may never see that New Testament model in our lifetime, but I want to work to break down as many of the man-made barriers as I can. I believe that the bride of Christ that is prepared for Christ's return is one that will not only be mature in character, but also in relationships. It will also be able to complete the task of the great commission with which we have been entrusted.
>
> All of this requires us to work together for the sake of the gospel and for the sake of 'speeding Christ's return'. At the age of nineteen, I was given a glimpse of the church as inclusive family, many-membered body, kingdom-advancing army, Spirit-filled temple, and glorious Christ-revealing bride. This has spoiled me for anything less. Since that day I have dreamed of 'the Church that Jesus died for and is coming back for'. It is what took me into, and then out of, a career

in medicine. It is what took me out of the comforts of the city of Bristol, and into the challenges of the amazing city of Liverpool. It is what gets me out of bed in the morning and keeps me awake at night. What else can I do?

Steve Botham lives in Birmingham, where he is director of the World Prayer Centre that recognises the importance of changing the spiritual climate in our towns and cities. Together with Gather, we are trying to develop a culture of prayer for our places; to encourage people to pray for God's blessing on key aspects of city and town life – its politics, health, business, media, arts, families and education and much more. He offers some wisdom on things he has learned about relating well with one another as we pray together from different Christian traditions:

Learn to be real and open. Love and respect each other. Support one another. It's a community before it's a movement.

Spend time on relationships. Unity is a long-term journey and it goes deeper the more we respect and understand each other.

Watch out for them and us – church leaders, para church leaders and other Christian leaders – this creates an unspoken defensiveness. We need to build kingdom. We need to make best use of everybody's skills and expertise.

Develop a strategic understanding, a desire to see large things happen.

Grow and nurture vision of what can be achieved and how we can deliver it.

Generous communication – we need to keep each other informed.

Team engagement; this is key, people commit to something when they have helped create it and feel a sense of ownership. We create a much better way forward when we have tapped into others' ideas and understanding.

Be open to disagreement. We are not building conformity but unity between lots of different views and backgrounds. When there is an open attitude to disagreement, people are much more likely to share what they feel and engage in robust discussion to get the best outcomes

Have clarity and focus; develop a clear understanding of our priorities, principles and next steps.

Andrew Belfield has recently formed the Mosaic Justice Network in Manchester, a collective of organisations working on social action with a desire to share information, initiate new ideas, solutions and partnerships together. With a Christian basis, they work with people across all faiths and none that offer various community programmes with an emphasis on social justice. They have found that, by getting to know one another and building strong relationships, they are able to navigate through the differences in their faith or working practices to express unity in diversity.

Andrew challenges us to look beyond the confines of the Church to build relationships and partnerships with others in our towns and cities that also seek the blessing and healing of their place, even if they don't share our religious beliefs:

I feel that we are faced with the greatest opportunity to stand up and be counted in this world which faces so much uncertainty and brokenness at this time. If we are prepared to sacrifice our labels and tribalism for the sake of true unity, the world will see the Church in increasing beauty. I am a believer of a better world and have tried to create contexts where this can occur intentionally and consistently and believe two is better than one. I believe if the Church concentrates more on getting the 'Found out' rather than getting the 'Lost in' we will see an amazing move of God in our nation.

Andy Taylor from Basingstoke also explains how growing friendships over teas and coffees with those from a different theological background has changed him:

Relationship is absolutely key to true unity. We have some extremely liberal church ministers in our town whom we would previously have had little or no contact [with], lobbing doctrinal grenades at each other from our trenches. I discovered that sitting down over a cup of coffee with some of these leaders, we discovered we had a lot more in common that we thought. We became friends and learned to listen to and trust each other, even though we disagreed over some issues.

I hope that we have established the need for unity, for growing partnerships with others and having a vision and strategy and a prayerful passion for the town or city God has sent you to serve. But how do we practically go about building relational gatherings in the place where we live? What tips can we learn from those who have already been praying and meeting together?

Some tips on forming a relational unity movement (by those who've done it)

1. One of the most difficult things is that it takes time, something that very few of us has enough of. But you can't rush relationships; pastoring a city is no different to pastoring a community, we must find the time to become a team, to eat and drink together, to play golf together, to meet one another's families, to trust one another until a deep sense of compassion and love is shared among us that dissolves ego and competition.

2. Start small, with leaders who want to meet regularly; better to begin with a small group of enthusiastic leaders than a larger group of half-hearted ones. Make sure your doors are always open to others; do not become exclusive and elitist.

3. Set the culture early on by being vulnerable and open with each other. This is not the time to show off or the opportunity to build your ego.

4. Make time to get to know other leaders and their families over coffee or food and be authentic, honest and real – not exaggerating or inflating stories.

5. Challenge leaders to see the strategic importance of the city above 'my patch', church or ministry. If they get the bigger vision, they will see their place in it alongside others.

6. Deliver a warm welcome to new churches, leaders and especially new people groups as they move in. Try to find time to meet them one to one to hear about their story and share about the culture you are growing in your meetings.

7. Culture is very deep! Don't blame others for theirs, rather ask them to appraise your own – you'll be challenged in the right places, learn more and deepen relationships far quicker. We all have parts of our cultures (including church cultures) which have to die, and some which form the unique charisma with which yours should bless the wider body of Christ.

8. Start by praying together and leave doctrinal differences to one side, other than a minimum shared Christology such as the Apostles' Creed.

9. Resist control and individual agendas from insecure leaders. Make sure the needs and opportunities of the city or town is the reason you meet together, and not people's pet projects.

10. Create a culture and environment that nurture and protect invention and fresh ideas.

11. People move between churches – and that is fine! Make sure you have an agreed system of open communication where those who seek to change church are asked to settle any unresolved issue with

the previous church. People will leave your church and others will come from other local churches to join yours; don't get unduly stressed.

Unity is one tune with one conductor and a multitude of instruments

How ridiculous would it be for an instrument in an orchestra to play their own favourite melody to their own rhythm without any reference to others. What a cacophony of sound it would create for each violin, cello, bassoon, timpani, trumpet to simply play whatever they wanted to without any reference to the given score and any acknowledgement of the conductor. And yet this is exactly what often happens in the church of God. Each local church, each denomination, each Christian charity does its own thing in its own way without reference to or conversation with others. We are indeed a cacophony of sound with little coordination or strategic outcomes. The conductor of the whole Church must be exasperated with us.

How much better for a wonderful celebration of diversity with each unique instrument playing its own score but part of the whole orchestral piece under the direction of the conductor who brings forward each at the right time in the right place. The violin is so very different and individual to the double bass, the piano is fundamentally distinctive from the oboe; however, when they come together to play the score in front of them under the direction of the conductor, they create a very beautiful sound. Each is made better by being part of something bigger; each is enhanced by the others when they play the right piece of music at the right time.

In responding to the needs of the city, we need to become an orchestra that is playing alongside one another, complementing each other, taking our part at the right moment to add to the overall score, to enhance what the writer and his conductor are seeking to achieve. If we can begin to do this across our cities and towns, instead of a cacophony, a beautiful melody will be heard across the town of the love of Christ.

Chapter 4
For the Love of God

Be still before the LORD and wait patiently for him ...
(Psalm 37:7)

Prayer is not asking. Prayer is putting oneself in the hands of
God, at His disposition, and listening to His voice in the depth
of our hearts. God shapes the world by prayer. The more
praying there is in the world the better the world will be, the
mightier the forces against the evil.
God speaks in the silence of the heart. Listening is the beginning
of prayer.
(Mother Teresa)

When the vision is to bless the city or town you have been
placed within, to work for it to be tangibly transformed
over a long period of time, it is no surprise that sustained
and passionate prayer is to be found at the heart of every
vibrant unity movement. With a vision so expansive and
challenging, there can be no other response but to seek God
for the resources, protection, empowering and grace
needed.

The way different cities and towns pray is very diverse and creative, but they all share one core belief, that they cannot do this without the power of God within and behind them. London Mission Collective have held prayer meetings at the top of the Shard, the highest building in London, One Heart One Voice Doncaster use a 24–7 prayer app on mobile phones, many cities meet every week early in the morning to seek God, others have gathered in cathedrals or warehouses, or prayer-walk the streets or around city walls. The form of prayer is multifaceted, allowing for different traditions and creative expressions, but the core unifying practice is that they believe that prayer changes things and their city or town can be slowly but surely transformed by calling on the God who loves our places to manifest His kingdom.

Prayer as small beginnings with great endings

There are many stories in the city transformation library where hundreds of people gather to call on God for their places, but perhaps the most accessible and inspiring of stories is where just two or three gather together faithfully praying for many years for God's hand and blessing to come and rest upon their town or city. Transformation takes time and perseverance, and those of us who are able to experience the joy of praying together in large gatherings need to be aware of the faithfulness of those who have gone before us and spent many years praying, often with tears, for change and unity to come.

Church growth and unity across Salford in Greater Manchester is now thriving. Some of the largest churches in the city have grown from small church plants, and pastors from all denominations meet and pray for one another regularly over lunch, where strong relationships have grown up. Although there is still much to be done, the journey towards spiritual, cultural and social transformation has begun in this once neglected city. Now home to Media City, where the BBC and more than 130 other media organisations broadcast their programmes daily, industry is thriving, the university is expanding and signs of regeneration are everywhere. But it wasn't always this way. Salford in the latter part of the twentieth century was a derelict port, a drug-ridden society run by several gangs who terrorised the area: educational attainment was very low, crime was very high and the Church was weak, small and divided.

As people increasingly sought to move out of the area in the 1960s, Pastor Bob King faithfully served and lived amid this broken community of Salford in his role of city missioner. He was known locally as 'Hero' because he stood up for the local people, praying for them, standing with them and living among them with his family. He remained in this place, trusting in the calling of God on his life, and loving the community, despite seeing little fruit in his forty years of service. But he sowed the seeds that are being harvested today, he paid a difficult price for remaining faithful and hidden in his prayers, and he remained firm. Sometimes the hardest enacted prayer is to simply stay where God has put you and stand for the values of His kingdom in a dark place. Any transformation that has arisen over the years across this great city was established on the vulnerability and faithfulness of people like Pastor King.

When his son David, who grew up in this hard urban environment, was called to ministry, he went to Bible college and was intent on serving God anywhere in the world in whatever difficult situation he might be placed, except in one place: Salford. Having seen his father's ministry produce so little fruit over such a long period of time, it was understandable that a change of scenery was called for. However, the call came to go back to Salford and Dave obeyed this call and set about building on his father's prayers and witness. After much serving and praying and particularly prayer-walking, Dave was given a word by God by the closed-down derelict docks which were for many years the centre of the industrial revolution, bringing in the raw materials for the local mills. Through decades of prayer and the faithful witness of his father, and through his own obedience, a word came that shaped his ministry and began the transformation. He felt God speak clearly that one day Salford would go to the world and the world would come to Salford. A future was spoken over this city, one place that was most unlikely to have a future; a new positive day was declared over a place where most people had given up.

From this prayerful leading, Dave and others began to believe, they began to speak well of the city and talk about its bright future. I remember Dave turning up to Manchester city leaders' meetings talking about what a wonderful place Salford was and the fantastic future it had. We all thought privately he was a bit mad or at least unrealistic. But then slowly but surely change began to happen, churches started to grow, Dave drew church leaders to come and pray together, a Christian police leader was appointed and a senior educationist took charge over the schools, education improved and crime started to fall. A Catholic businessman started to invest in the area, buying the docks and founding Media City. Salford has moved from being a place you wanted to move out of to being desirable location; churches want to plant in the city and media companies from around the world are arriving. The world is coming to Salford and Salford is having an impact on the world.

A similar story of long-term faithful praying leading to wider impact is found in Sunderland. Once named as one of the largest ship-building cities in the world, the industrial north-east coastal city of Sunderland has experienced much unemployment over the past thirty years, with the decline of many of its industries due to overseas competition. The closing of coal mines, shipyards and glass factories have meant changing lifestyles for many, and recovery has been slow, the car industry now being the major supplier of work. Amid this declining community, a lady called Florence Brown and her husband, David, were filled with the Spirit in 1970 and began to feel God's heart for their place. They started to pray for the spiritual, social and cultural regeneration of their beloved city of Sunderland.

Deb Fozzard, who now leads the Sunderland Connect Network, says:

We have grown through the favour of God and the prayers of the generations past and present who have faithfully prayed and sown into Sunderland.

Deb launched the Connect Network on 8th June 2015 at the Stadium of Light, bringing every denomination and tradition together: Methodist, Catholic, URC, Baptist, Pentecostal, Anglican alongside different organisations working with families, addicts, schools and other community groups. There are currently forty-eight leaders, including chaplains, actively engaging in the social and spiritual transformation of Sunderland who are now meeting together and praying for their city.

One of the most mature and long-standing expressions of unity movements in the UK is found in York, where a couple of ministers met to pray together for the revival of this great city. York, a historic walled city in the north-east of England, founded by the Romans, has a strong Christian history. In the 2011 census 59.5 per cent of residents considered themselves Christian. Graham Hutchinson, one of the church leaders in the city, explains how a spirit of unity has continued to flourish and that their weekly leaders' prayer meeting began in 1999 without a name or plans as to how long it would continue:

> Two church leaders had a conversation, one who had just arrived in the city and one having been in York for a while. I suggested that the two of us meet from time to time to pray for the city. 'Give me a few days,' the other one said. He phoned around and about five leaders, from various churches, gathered to pray for

the city. At first it was supposed to be monthly but after two months it was decided to move to weekly.

The ground rules were that no one would talk (brag) about their own church to avoid competitiveness, that prayer matters that could be dealt with in their own churches should be saved for there, and that we would pray for our city.

More church leaders and leaders of Christian ministries started to come along and the regular attendance grew. Some of those people were from an existing network in the city called One Voice York.

One Voice York was born after churches in the area became excited about working together in mission in 1990 and was typical of what was happening in various locations in the UK at that time. The York churches had first come together to organise a live link event in the minster when Billy Graham was in Sheffield. Satellite pictures were displayed on giant screens in the minster. Thousands attended. Many came to faith. In the years that followed prayer breakfasts happened from time to time, there was involvement in the Make Way movement of city centre and neighbourhood marches. Then in January 2000 Chris Cullwick and John Young led a group of fifty on a One Voice pilgrimage to the Holy Land to start the new millennium where it all began.

The prayer meeting and One Voice merged and the One Voice York prayer meeting now takes place for one hour every Wednesday morning from 7.45am to 8.45am, followed by a toast and spreads breakfast. Attendance is currently thirty to forty-five people, with more at the monthly meetings when the full-time church youth workers join, and lead, the meeting. Many denominations are represented: Pentecostal, Methodist, Church of England, Roman Catholic, Baptist, various 'new' churches, Black Majority Pentecostal, various Christian ministries and charities.

Because of the regular prayer, including those who are not able to be very regular, we have grown good relationships which make for efficient working together when we decide to work on a project together.

The churches in Reading share a similar story. A large town on the Thames and Kennet rivers, west of London in southern England, it has a long history with Anglo-Saxon beginnings. Now an important commercial centre, the town is home to the headquarters of a number of significant companies as well as being considered a part of the London commuter belt. The Reading Christian Network (RCN), made up of leaders of churches and Christian organisations, have met weekly for prayer and to build relationships together since 1997 following a challenge from evangelist Ed Silvoso, who led a conference in the town, for the wider Church to take responsibility to be a blessing to the Reading area. Steve Prince, one of the leaders of the RCN, says:

We now have between forty to sixty leaders of churches and charities meeting to pray every week. People come from a wide variety of streams – Baptist, Anglican, Pentecostal, Salvation Army, Charismatic free churches etc. In the early years there were fewer church leaders from more traditional backgrounds, who related together under the banner of Churches Together in Reading, but over the years those boundaries have blurred considerably with many choosing to pray and meet with us, including some from Catholic, Methodist and more conservative evangelical churches.

We have a good number of black and other minority ethnic leaders in our numbers, including key members of the leadership team, but are aware that there is more to do in our highly diverse town (with around 150 languages spoken by children in our schools, as an indicator).

The balance between congregational leaders and leaders of other (mainly social action) ministries has also shifted considerably over time, with a much more even split now. Similarly with the gender balance – while not equal in numbers, there are considerably more women who meet with us now.

People attending the leaders' prayer [meeting] are leaders of churches or Christian organisations from Reading and the surrounding areas. This includes senior leaders and members of leadership teams from churches and those who are encouraged to attend by a member of their church leadership team. Similarly, leaders and directors of organisations and charities may invite people from their leadership teams to attend. We ask that everyone attending is part of a local church and can commit to our vision of the transformation of Reading through the life, love and power of Jesus Christ.

Faith for the kingdom to come is always referred to in the Bible as starting small, and seemingly insignificant. That implies waiting – being patient and willing to serve faithfully in our communities and to wait until God moves rather than rush ahead with our own plans, projects and agendas. Transformation of our towns and cities takes time and it is always birthed in prayer.

Prayer as a humble attitude

Long-term sustained prayer for our places is not a strategy to be conducted, but a posture to be developed, an attitude of heart that places God at the centre of all things: 'To whom shall we go? You have the words of eternal life' (John 6:68). Humility begins and sustains all prayer for our places. Humility is the call 'to walk humbly with [our] God' (Micah 6:8), to relate to the very creator of our places, to follow God's leading to pray into effect the will and vision of God's kingdom. Humility puts us in our rightful place and God on the throne; it creates in us the desire and the need to call out to this throne for the answers and resources to see places transformed.

In October 2001 the national Experian report, a secular study exploring the socio-economic indicators in 376 towns and cities, declared the city of Stoke the worst place to live in England. This began an amazing journey of humility, repentance and prayer across the churches and leaders of the area based on the 2 Chronicles 7:14 passage, 'If my people, who are called by my name, will humble themselves and pray and seek my face and turn from their wicked ways, then I will hear from heaven, and I will forgive their sin and will heal their land.' Lloyd Cooke, who heads a charity called Saltbox, tells us:

In a spirit of honesty and vulnerability, there was a recognition that the area was in dire spiritual, political and economic need. The church leaders observed that churches in the area were struggling both spiritually and numerically, and that many church leaders were themselves discouraged and under pressure. In the light of these desperate times and the Experian report, the leaders prayed together expressing a desire to see a new spirit of support and encouragement, and asking God for a transformation of the area. So they set a date for prayer meeting 31st October 2001.

Prior to the evening of Wednesday 31st October, and because of the lack of publicity, only about fifty to eighty were expected. Amazingly, over 200 people turned up! Alongside this surprising attendance, the meeting contained a real sense of the Lord's presence. As leaders from the morning meeting shared their heart, there was real honesty and a willingness to admit our failings and difficulties. Sharing, worship and prayer was interweaved throughout the evening, with various types of creative praying being employed. The key scripture for the evening was 2 Chronicles 7:14.

At one point, a local church leader came forward to offer a public apology for any past hurt or offence that his congregation may have caused. Other leaders also came forward and humbled themselves before the Lord. This united act of submission and repentance powerfully affected those attending. As the evening came to a conclusion, it became apparent that follow-up was necessary and so a second meeting was announced that would take place on the last day of November. There was a real sense that something very significant had just begun. Churches across the area began to think and pray for the wider needs of their city and not just their congregation. Regular city-wide prayer gatherings brought about a greater sense of unity creating strategic connections in various sectors like business, education, health, politics etc. Their cry of repentance was to ask for forgiveness that on their watch, this had happened and to ask God to hear their cries and to restore his favour and blessing to the streets and homes, the businesses and industries and even the local football club.

As I mentioned earlier, following this increased movement of prayer, the Christians in Stoke began to focus their prayers, with some very specific goals. They not only prayed for an increase in the harvest – for increasing numbers of people to come to faith in Christ. They prayed that God would release healing power on people, families, congregations and the land; for improvements in business education, health, law, media and arts, politics. They called on God for continued government investment and a reduction in crime and the fear of crime. They prayed for high-profile visionary leadership, improved educational attainments, change in the local 'victim mentality', cranes on the city centre skyline as a sign of growth, and for Stoke City football team to gain entry into the Premiership (leading to improved morale). Many of these prayer requests have or are being answered, with perhaps the highlight being that in 2008 Stoke City FC gained entry into the Premier League and has never been relegated yet.

In Birmingham, a large multicultural city in the heart of the Midlands, there have been many varied expressions of prayer and attempts at growing unity across the churches, but for many years there was little fruit. However, a tragic event in 2010 triggered a renewed desire for the churches to come together in humility, to put aside their differences and pray and serve their city together. Steve Botham from Birmingham's World Prayer Centre explains:

> You could say our story begins with George Cadbury bringing hundreds of church leaders together to pray together and organise a mission in Birmingham to reach 600,000 people in 1896. Unity has ebbed and flowed in our city but there have been many great movements of God when thousands gave their lives to Jesus.
>
> Our present unity comes out of the riots in 2010. As is so often the case, we pray when we are desperate, and Birmingham faced a dark threat when three young Asian men were deliberately killed by a car driven by Afro-Caribbean young men in the frenzied climate of riots and protecting territories. Words soon circulated that the Asian youth were incensed and were preparing for a night when they would attack the Afro-Caribbean community and take more lives. The city braced itself for mayhem and possibly a deep breakdown in community relations. Many Christians prayed for peace and out

stepped Tariq Jahan, father of one of the boys; in a dignified challenge he told the young men to stand down. The community leaders gathered that night with the police and local politicians. Christians were very much in the minority but a local Elim minister made the most telling contribution, challenging the faith leaders to lead and bring about peace. At the end of the week there was a remarkable multi-faith gathering in the park near the spot where the three young men died and we were able to speak peace and work at unity. The Church and church leaders were very prominent and a number of us spoke to the assembled communities.

This event brought different church, business and prayer leaders together and made us realise there was no united prayer gathering in the city and there needed to be one. The Elim minister, Mark Ryan, volunteered to host a monthly event, and a group of about fifty met to pray for the still bruised and tense city. Those regular gatherings are now in their seventh year and have been called 'For the city' and have also birthed a number of cross-city activities and city-wide prayer meetings.

Prayer as celebration and declaration

Prayer for our places often begins in humble, small ways, but it certainly can grow to be expressed in large-scale gatherings of the body of Christ across a city or town, declaring the love of God for the area. Many city- and town-based unity movements have had large prayer and celebration events, declaring their unity and interceding for the area.

Chris Cottee of Christians Across Watford describes their annual summertime open air band stand celebrations:

> On a grey but warm Sunday morning in July, some 600 Christians from churches and fellowships of all traditions in Watford gather expectantly at the bandstand by the town hall at the top end of the town for our annual 'bandstand service', as it's now become known. In [the] early years, back in the 1990s, it was held in Cassiobury Park. The newer venue gets us better public exposure as we give witness to the unity of Christ's one Church in Watford and for Watford.
>
> Together we experience times of joyful, Christ-centred worship, led by a band in the shelter of the bandstand; then to prayers, readings, a confession, and a children's activity, all directed by leaders from churches of varying traditions. It is truly uplifting to see a charismatic Pentecostal and a Roman Catholic priest sharing the same stage in true love and harmony.
>
> And the point of all this preparation, energy, time and prayer? From long ago, back in the 1990s, when the Spirit of Jesus first called us to set aside other priorities for the task of expressing the unity He has given us, we felt that some sort of big, annual demonstration of that unity was important – that we should cancel our own services that morning, where possible, and dedicate ourselves to a shared celebration of Christ. This would not only express,

but also strengthen, that unity and enlarge our vision for it. It would encourage members of small churches to see the bigger picture – what we are part of together. It would give visible credibility to our claim that in God's eyes we are one Church, in Watford and for Watford. But one thing we didn't expect back then was that the very act of worshipping together in this way would have a spiritual impact 'in the heavenlies'. We have become convinced that something changes over us, and over our town, when we celebrate Christ in this way.

Unity and prayer really work – the best testimony of this came from our still-elected mayor, Dorothy Thornhill: now a Baroness and with a broad view of all things that have happened in Watford, in January 2017 she attended our CAW Residential at High Leigh. She said that the unity and prayers of the Christians in Watford had formed a 'shield' over the town. She said that this has changed the atmosphere in Watford and made 'goodness' normal in the town, unlike other neighbouring towns.

Art Ellinson from Wrexham in North Wales believes that collective worship from a wide expression of the gathered Church is really important for their place, but also shares how this has sometimes been difficult to achieve:

It is wonderful when Christians from different traditions can worship together, expectant that their worship could lead to spiritual renewal. It needs an acceptance that different forms of worship are valid and that it is permissible and potentially beneficial and enjoyable to embrace them from time to time.

While the vast majority of worship services will take place in individual congregations, and take place in the 'style' used by that congregation, it is important that on a number of occasions each year, the town witnesses large-scale worship gatherings when Christians of the various traditions are found together at ease, and engaged in purposeful creative worship. What is purposeless is a bland form of worship, searching for a lowest common denominator, delivered without a helpful hand. Thoughtless application of liturgy, rigid adherence to a chapel hymn/prayer/preach sandwich format, or a lack of preparation on the pretence of 'spontaneity' being the only valid approach, are unlikely to be helpful ...

Helping a united congregation into new and different forms of worship is a great gift, and helping congregations from different traditions to be sensitive to one another yet also adventuresome is so important. I believe it's difficult and rarely are local churches successful in having truly united large-scale worship services engaging a broad cross-section of the Church in the town, embracing those who normally worship in a contemplative mode, and also those whose worship is usually exuberant.

In the Roman city of Bath in the south-west of England, many hundreds of people come to their central prayer events. Sir Peter Heywood, who set up Bath Christian Action Network, explains:

We hold a Pray for Bath evening at Bath Abbey twice a year, bringing people together from the Christian community, to pray together for the city, and to hear from the council, the police, the health service, the university etc about their requests for prayer.

We issue our Pray for Bath booklet at the beginning of Lent each year, with a focus for prayer about an aspect of the city on each day of Lent. This year, 2017, we distributed 10,000 copies and started Lent with a Prayer Tent on the main pedestrian thoroughfare in the city centre for eleven days. We built some enormous containers out of metal mesh, and then people popped a coloured ball into the relevant container for each prayer made in the street, red = thank you, blue = please, brown = sorry and orange = a prayer for the city.

People from many of our churches staffed the tent. Many hundreds of people stopped and prayed.

It's not about ecumenical groupings, or just gathering church leaders together, but about Christians living, serving and worshipping together, whichever church they come from.

Our aim is to make it easier for the Church in Bath to talk with the council, police and other authorities. We love to see people's mind-sets changing, as individuals in the authorities realise that engaging with the Church is a great thing.

And flowing from this is encouraging Christians to join together in social action projects to address the needs in our city, working in cooperation with the council.

We encourage all Christians in Bath to be serving their community and taking responsibility for the city. Our dream is that each church in Bath becomes a place where Christians are taught, refuelled and then sent out to bless the people and places around them.

Other places pray collectively and express their unity as one Church across their town or city through new and creative expressions of the more traditional Whit Walks or prayer marches. Colourful banners, guitars and music, or the carrying of large crosses bring many different denominations together to give witness to God's love for their places.

Andy Glover from Chester who leads Link Up – the unity movement for Christians across Chester and West Cheshire – describes how together they celebrate the Easter story through the medieval streets of Chester with a Passion Play, to sit alongside the cities Mystery Plays:

On the morning of Good Friday 2017 you couldn't walk up Eastgate Street to Chester Cross for the crowds. But this wasn't because of shoppers out for an early bird bargain, but the city centre streets of Chester thronged with 3,500 people to witness the performance of the City Passion Play. Hundreds of volunteer actors, singers and children told the story of the last days of the life of Jesus with the city's heritage, shops and glorious cathedral providing the backdrop to one of life's best-known stories.

Under a clouded sky, spectators witnessed Jesus enter the city through the Eastgate Clock arch before being welcomed by fans and followers waving palm fronds and the drums of Karamba Samba at Chester Cross. On the historic rows Caiaphas and Annas charge him with blasphemy before sending him to trial at the Town Hall Square. The Last Supper was also on the 'Rows' strategically located above the café in Browns of Chester, while the steps of St Peter's Church was the setting for the Garden of Gethsamane. Jesus' road to Calvary was a short distance to Chester Cathedral, here the crowd fell silent for the moving scene of the crucifixion as Matt Baker's 'Yet Hope I', described by Prince Charles on a visit to the city in 2014 as 'intensely beautiful', resounded around the area in front of the famous West Door.

I happened to be standing next to the vice-dean of Chester Cathedral as people came up to us both to congratulate us on the performance, saying things like: 'I have never been so moved', 'I have never seen Chester like this', 'the best thing I have ever seen in the city'.

I had the privilege of being the chair of the steering group that pulled together for twelve weeks to plan and produce what we eventually called the 'City Passion Play'. Around the table were church leaders from Chester Cathedral, a local Methodist church, a Quaker, a 'new church stream' leader, a pioneer curate who helps lead a local theatre group called B-It Theatre Company, and me, a Baptist minister. We represented Churches Together in Chester and Link Up. With us was Jo Sykes, the chair of the Chester Mystery Plays and Matt Baker, the director of a local theatre company called Theatre in the Quarter. The Chester Mystery Plays form a spectacular festival presented mainly by members of the local community under professional direction. They are performed in Chester every five years, with the most recent production being in 2013 in the nave of Chester Cathedral and the next full production being planned for 2018. Matt ... is Chester born and bred and is a multitalented composer, arranger and performer; he also worked with the Chester Mystery Play to produce the 2013 play. Without Jo and Matt's involvement we would never had produced such a high-quality play and performance.

The cast and chorus were drawn from the local churches, the local community and from previous cycles of the Chester Mystery Plays. They were joined by Karamba Samba, a community samba band based in Chester, the local soldiers from Roman Tours, the town crier, David Mitchell and Lucius the donkey! The City Passion Play was a wonderful example of partnership not ownership, one of the values of Link Up; it could never have been performed if just one organisation or church had tried to do it, we also had people of faith, no faith and some faith all working together ... [7]

Liverpool, the large northern city known for its music industry and football teams, developed a major prayer initiative launched in 2009 called Continuous Prayer, with a chain of churches each taking responsibility for praying during a week in the year. Nic Harding says:

---

[7] Check out https://youtu.be/kneisRLccH4 for a nine-minute video of the play.

Churches prayed in their own style and to their own timetable. Some actually organised a 24–7 prayer week, another included prayer walking in the neighbourhood and visiting homes to ask for prayer requests. The unifying activity was the baton, consisting of a prayer diary in which the praying church recorded what it had done and answers to prayers seen, that was handed on from one church to the next at the end of the week. This continued for seven years and was a great encouragement to unity with many stories of blessing coming out of it.

An Anglican church produced a paper chain with each link representing a prayer. They produced a video showing the chain draping the sanctuary, and at the end of the week went to the next church in line (a Brethren church) and showed the video in the morning worship. The church was deeply moved when the vicar said that the final link was the prayer that they prayed for them.

After a couple of years of this it was further developed by asking each church to focus their prayers on the next church in line. A numerically small church in north Liverpool were asked to pray for a much larger Pentecostal church on the Wirral. They went over to the area where the church was located and prayer-walked the streets. On the Sunday, the day of handing over the baton, they carried a financial offering for them, and shared a verse of Scripture that God had given them for the Pentecostal church, which turned out to be the very scripture that the pastor was speaking on that day.

Bob Bain and his wife, Mary, from east London have a passion for prayer-walking around the boundaries of the place God has called them to serve. They have lived in Havering, on the edge of one of London's thirty-two boroughs, for the past eight years and felt God ask them to call the churches to 'sing out a new song' over their community.

Firstly we were to map the place from God's perspective and pick out the highest points in the borough. We felt that God was saying 'sing from the mountaintop' in a prophetic releasing way, proclaiming God's kingdom has come, and we would be given the anointing to do this task. Jesus was inviting us to join in the declaring out of His commission, and this would be our commission too. In the words of Luke chapter 4, 'The Spirit of the Lord is upon me because he has anointed me to proclaim good news to the poor. He has sent me to proclaim freedom for the prisoners and recovery of sight for the blind, to set the oppressed free, to proclaim the year of the Lord's favour' [4:18-19].

We were being called to take the 'high places', the places in opposition to God … In the late afternoon of Sunday 7th June 2015, seventy to eighty representative worshippers, pray-ers and prophets sang at eight different locations around the London Borough of Havering. My wife, Mary, and I were two of them. Our vision to sing over Havering had become a reality! The pace of the Holy Spirit is such that a date, only a short while back, can seem like pre-history, but God holds all our tears in a bottle and numbers the days and the years, and we believe that this date goes down as a significant one.

We chose certain places from which the groups would sing, declare and pray. This doesn't mean that there aren't other significant places in the borough, but just that these were the 'high places' which God highlighted for us on this particular occasion.

I have yet to find a vibrant movement of unity for the sake of mission that has not been birthed and sustained in prayer. Reaching our towns, cities, boroughs and islands is not ultimately about activity, strategy and effort, it is about a deep reliance on the power and activity of God in the midst of the places He has created. We are ultimately unable to transform anything. We are constantly fighting against ingrained negative cultural attitudes; we find ourselves dealing with the sinfulness of greed, pride and power. We are facing significant social, environmental and cultural challenges that challenge even the most talented and resourceful of governments. Yes, we are better placed if we operate as one body, if we enable our members to be city-changers in their spheres of activity and we become more strategic and coordinated. However, even with all that going for us, the task of city and town transformation is ultimately beyond us. I struggle to effect any small-scale personal change yet alone major social, cultural and spiritual transformation.

However, with faith expressed through prayer, we being to tap into the most powerful force in the universe. We begin to listen to the heart of God for our places, we begin to speak out and act out that heart in specific and sustained ways. We begin not to trust in our own strength or in our own might and power but in the power and activity of the Holy Spirit.

It is through prayer in the God of creation, salvation and resurrection that we will see change, people's lives turned around, cultures developing and social contexts improved.

Chapter 5
For the Love of Our Places

As he approached Jerusalem and saw the city, he wept over it.
(Luke 19:41)

One of the key hallmarks of these vibrant unity movements alongside a focus on prayer and a commitment to relational unity is the overall purpose of God's transformative mission towards the city or town. If the body of Christ only expresses itself in building strong relationships and praying together, it will over time run out of passion and purpose. If prayer is the bow and relationships are the shaft and feathers, then mission is the arrowhead. At the beginning of Acts of the Apostles, the early Church responded to the movement of the Holy Spirit in prayer by seeking God for empowering and guidance, and it also expressed the gospel in building an extraordinary relational community that was able to share all its possessions. However, the overwhelming energy, purpose and vision was to spread the good news of Christ's resurrection and offer of reconciliation across the Roman Empire.

Van Rheen expresses this missional purpose of the Church, saying:

> Mission is the very lifeblood of the church. As the body cannot survive without blood, so the church cannot survive without mission. Without blood the body dies; without mission the church dies. As the physical body becomes weak without sufficient oxygen-carrying red blood cells, so the church becomes anaemic if it does not express its faith. The church … establishes its rationale for being—its purpose for existing—while articulating its faith. An unexpressed faith withers. A Christian fellowship without mission loses its vitality. Mission is the force that gives the body of Christ vibrancy, purpose, and direction. When the church neglects its role as God's agent for mission, it is actually neglecting its own lifeblood.[8]

The transformational missions work undertaken by these unity movements can roughly be subdivided into three expressions of mission.

1. *Spiritual transformation*, relating to the personal transformation in people's lives, which is the work of evangelism; as the declaration of God's word and the process of discipleship. (Using the word 'spiritual' is in some ways inaccurate since all things are spiritual in the kingdom of God, and we must reject a dualistic

---

[8] Gailyn Van Rheenen, *Missions: Biblical Foundations and Contemporary Strategies* (Grand Rapids, MI: Zondervan, 1996), p31.

viewpoint. However, for the sake of differentiation with the other three expressions of mission, it is easier to use.)

2. *Social transformation,* where the outworking of the good news across society is that the hungry are fed, the thirsty are given water, the homeless are housed, the vulnerable are protected and the poor are lifted up. This social transformation also asks the hard questions about why the poor are poor and why the vulnerable end up abused. Social transformation is as much about a social justice as it is about social service.

3. *Cultural transformation,* where we seek to disciple the nations and by default their cities in the ways and thinking of the kingdom of God. Cultural transformation is about developing kingdom values, ways of thinking and new social norms. Jesus spent a lot of time critiquing the culture of His day with its elitism, materialism and a belief that violence was redemptive. A number of unity movements are beginning to ask the question for their city or town, how can we disciple this place in the values of compassion, forgiveness, truth, love and justice? Can we think and therefore act in a less materialistic and elitist way, and place a greater value on stewardship and equality? Can we build dependent communities rather than continue on in the values of isolated independence?

> The mission of the Christian community in Acts is a mission of salvation, as was the work of Jesus. Salvation involves the reversal of all the evil consequences of sin, against both God and

neighbour. It does not have only a 'vertical' dimension.[9]

While unity movements are at different stages with different emphases, the more mature ones, those particularly who have been active for over twenty years, such as RCN, are expressing transformation in its more roundest sense. Their leadership team reflect on the breadth of transformation that has and is occurring in Reading in the south of England:

> We have experienced increasing favour and have established good working relationships with a variety of strategic groups, including the local authority, police, MPs and others who have influence in and across the geographical area we represent.
>
> Through our network there are multiple connections across churches, organisations, individuals with common gifting, local areas within the town, employees engaged in all sorts of companies and public services. Without our visible presence as a combined group, much of this would either not happen or do so at a much lower level: our unity creates the environment in which such connections and relationships can multiply and grow in number and effectiveness.
>
> By being visible to the civic authorities, we can open up conversations and relationships that produce fruit in terms of how we represent Jesus in

[9] David J Bosch, *Transforming Mission: Paradigm Shifts in Theology of Mission* (20th Anniversary Edition) (Maryknoll, NY: Orbis Books, 2011), p192.

loving and serving our communities as authentic servants of the gospel.

It also challenges our own attitudes of independence and isolationism; mixing with others who love and serve the same Jesus with different theologies, cultures and practices tests our hearts and forces us to think through what true unity looks and feels like.

We see a Church that makes no distinction between the 'sacred and the secular' or between the validity and significance of roles whether primarily exercised in supporting and equipping the Church or in acts of kindness and compassion in specific areas of society.

We embrace the apostolic, missional, sending nature of who we are called to be as the Church in the town or city. We believe the gospel of Jesus Christ is good news to all and we see our ultimate mission as communicating and demonstrating this to all through our actions and words.

We believe God's heart is to remove the isolation and aloneness of individual people and to place them in physical and spiritual families, where they may experience the completeness and reality of God's love restoring them physically, spiritually and emotionally. We will work together to encourage one another to be good news and to eliminate systemic poverty – physically, spiritually and emotionally.

We will affirm, enable and equip Christians to exercise their callings and gifts in appropriate and connected contexts – often through specialist

Christian organisations whose leaders and people are genuinely part of a local church.

Spiritual transformation

At the heart of any sustainable social and cultural change over an area there must at the core be a fundamental change in the behaviours and attitudes of the residents of that area. The gospel of Jesus speaks powerfully into this need by its offer of a new life, a new beginning, a conversion, a turning around towards the ways of the kingdom of God. It's good news because it is made possible by the actions of God in Christ Jesus, Who came to take all that is not of God, all that hinders change, community and justice, to Himself on the cross and Who defeated its power over us in the resurrection. In Christ God declares a new day to this world: 'The message of Easter is that God's new world has been unveiled in Jesus Christ and that you're now invited to belong to it.'[10] The declaration of this new day, the sharing of this event through evangelism is crucial to the overall transformation of society and the future coming of God's kingdom.

So each of us is called to give account of the hope that is within us, to live and demonstrate the good news and where appropriate to share faith with others, calling them to follow this transforming God. We are to do this personally and corporately as local churches with wisdom, gentleness, love and boldness. However, if we begin to express ourselves as the one body of Christ across a city or

---

[10] N T Wright, *Surprised by Hope: Rethinking Heaven, the Resurrection, and the Mission of the Church* (New York: HarperOne, 2008), pp352-353.

town, then the possibilities for sharing of resources and the subsequent increasing impact are considerable. It's good for one church to engage in evangelistic mission but it's at another level of impact when all the churches do it across an area for an extended time.

Christians across Watford in 2016 held a week-long mission called 'The Gospel According to Mark (Ritchie)'. Tim Roberts, one of the leaders, explains:

> We were working in partnership with the evangelist and we welcomed over 1,000 people to eleven different proclamation evangelistic events in nine venues in a week, and saw many people make first-time commitments to Christ. It allowed many different churches to host the event in an authentic way to their tradition, provide their own musical entertainment, and then provide a platform for Mark to present the gospel. It was a great success.

The churches in Greater Manchester held two very successful city-wide missions in 2000 and 2002 led by the Message Trust that drew together large numbers of churches to reach particularly the young people of the city. More recently in Reading, through the ministry of Yinka Oyekan, The Turning has become a significant unity-led evangelistic missions opportunity.

> On the 29th of May 2016 we began what we thought would be a one-week mission at our Baptist Church 'The Gate' which would possibly stretch into two weeks. In the end because of the results we were witnessing on the streets we stretched out the

mission for a total of four weeks. In that time, we saw over 1850 people prayed for on the streets of Reading with many first-time commitments and rededications to Christ. Quite apart from the large numbers of responses to the gospel the sheer number of people willing to let us pray for them on the streets took us by surprise.

Seven months on from The Turning outpouring that shook our church in Reading, we have been excited to see in practice that this grace can and has been released in other cities. We have gained much insight through conducting five months of mission which has culminated in seeing over 4150 people in England and at last count over 865 in Lille in France respond in prayer to an invitation to accept Christ.

In the UK leadership teams covering over 230 towns and cities have asked us to bring The Turning to their town or city. In England, we are calling the implementation of this campaign to bring The Turning to these places 'The Big Bang', a campaign that will be inviting cities and towns to receive the best training we can give them prior to launching a Turning Team in their city or town. We will also be launching a similar event in several other countries in Europe where we have invitations to bring The Turning.

This joint strategic and coordinated evangelism has been an ongoing activity across Chester through the unity movement, Link Up. Andy Glover explains some of the breadth of activities over a number of years:

Chester churches worked together from 2005 through to 2009 on Chesterfest. In 2007 our 'summer celebration week' has twenty-one church partners plus organisations who partnered with us including Christian and public sector bodies. We have 150 youth involved all from Chester plus forty youth leaders, Yfriday joined us for the week and we ran twenty-four CAKE (Community Acts of Kindness Experience) Projects. There was also an Adult Programme with over 170 delegates, forty to fifty coming together each day for worship and teaching and then CAKE projects in the afternoons. We held evening outreach events and youth events at the cathedral with Yfriday as the main act which attracted over 500 young people. Funday on a Sunday that year had over 9,000 visitors and over 300 volunteers involved, staffing all the activities. In 2008 and 2009 we held similar 'summer celebration weeks' including the Funday on a Sunday which in 2009 had nearly 12,000 visitors.

These are just some of the many examples of evangelistic ministry that the power of working together as one body can produce. Numerous joint city-wide Alpha courses have been run, and the evangelist J.John has carried out successful missions linking with unity movements across cities. Many cities have regular Party in the Park events, summer festivals and Christmas outreaches. Hope Together since its beginnings in 2008 has produced numerous resources and has been able to support many church unity movements in doing joined-up evangelism focusing on the rhythm of the year from Easter to Pentecost from summer events to harvest celebrations on to the Christmas period.

Together for the Harvest across Liverpool have always had an emphasis on evangelism, with their vision statement declaring that their goal is to reach every man, woman and child in the Liverpool city region with the gospel in the next ten years. They go on to explain:

> Imagine what our Mersey region would look like in ten years' time if every man, woman and child had experienced a vibrant expression of the gospel – something they saw demonstrated in our lives and relationships; but had also heard and understood a message of hope for their lives. Imagine our neighbourhoods, our families, our workplaces transformed with changed lives. Imagine tens of thousands of people coming to faith, affecting those around them, and infecting the culture of our city region.

Now with fresh vision and new leadership, TFH is setting the ambitious goal of reaching every person in our region in the next ten years. To do this we need every church involved. Every church owning God's heart for the lost. Every church demonstrating and declaring the good news.

It was a blessing to work together with many churches in 2001 and to hold ten meetings at the Liverpool Anglican Cathedral for the just10 mission with J.John. A team of about twelve people drawn from different churches, traditions and geographical locations was commissioned to organise and run this. Attendance was over 1,000 people each night and several hundred people responded to the appeals for salvation. This was part of the 'mobilisation' aspect of the TFH vision that also resulted in an increase in unity between churches.

TFH worked closely with Festival Manchester, employing one leader part-time to inform people about it and encourage their support. It resulted in over 600 people booking in for the week-long festival of worship, teaching and community projects. Two years later we organised our own version, called Merseyfest. Two thousand people camped in a Liverpool park and 200 community projects were completed across the region, with multiple evangelistic events each evening. It ended with a weekend festival, with police estimates of 75,000 people attending on the two days. There were many answers to prayer, particularly in building relationships with Liverpool borough council, who initially were unenthusiastic about the event but ended up being supportive. It has resulted in a more positive attitude towards the Church in the region. In total over 200 churches were involved in it.

Another approach has been the ministry of healing as an opportunity to express God's grace across a city; this ministry has been a particular focus for Birmingham churches. Linda Isgrove from the city explains:

We started with three churches working together on Healing Rooms and two churches with Healing on the Streets (HOTS). We now have eleven sites in Birmingham for 'HOTS' plus Healing Rooms and a chaplaincy group who pray at the children's hospital.

The three city centre sites have teams made up of Christians from a number of churches including a large number of Muslim background believers. Other teams are individual churches or a mixture. Churches that vary with Anglicans, Baptist, Vineyard, Independents involved.

Social transformation

Since the financial crisis in 2008, unprecedented opportunities have arisen for churches to respond to the significant reduction in funding for statutory services. With the majority of local authorities having to reduce their services by up to 50 per cent from previous levels, anything that is not a legal requirement has either been significantly reduced or stopped altogether. Churches are well placed to respond to the needs as one of the few third-sector organisations that weren't on the whole reliant on outside grant funding. We have been reflecting that churches are much more able to pool resources when they work in a strategic and coordinated way; this is very apparent when it comes to delivery of social services to the community. Peter McClellan, a key leader in Durham, reflects on this approach that has been operating very effectively:

> County Durham is home to a prestigious university, glorious landscapes and the poverty associated with the closure of one of the largest coalfields in England. Rivalry between villages and pits has left a legacy of tribalism and division which is all too often reflected in the Church. Over the last few years those church divisions are slowly breaking down as God draws

people together and turns their attention outwards to the very real needs of our communities.

Durham Christian Partnership has been growing over the last four years as an umbrella body for a number of projects, operating first in Durham city and now across County Durham. It now provides training and conferences, a listening service in Durham Cathedral, StreetLights (a Street Pastor-style service), a grandparents' support group, a debt advice service and food bank. The food bank operates across County Durham with twenty-five distribution points and 15,000 clients in the last twelve months. It especially has been a catalyst for Church unity and involves people from over 100 churches working together. This is starting to break down inter-church boundaries and surprises everyone with the unity possible when we focus outwards towards our neighbours. With the impact of the food bank has come increased partnership working with other charities and meaningful engagement with the police, health services and the local authority. Willing volunteers are in demand as cuts bite deep into services and the Christian label is no longer a problem. Opportunities are everywhere and resources from secular grant-making bodies are accessible as we expand our services – including the welcome news this week of a grant of almost £400,000 for the food bank and associated support services over the next three years.

We see God's provision as we've sought to love and serve our communities. We pray for increased unity and for a deepening of the love between our various church families and for even more opportunities to share Jesus through our words and actions.

Another city whose churches have been very effective over the years in social action is Southampton, known historically for its bustling trading port and jobs creation and as the place from where the *Titanic* set forth. Despite its illustrious reputation, the city with prosperity coming through its docks has experienced more recent setbacks. Alongside higher levels of employment insecurity, the local authority in Southampton is facing a serious funding crisis. Programmes are under threat, something which could spell a future with no libraries, youth clubs, repaired potholes or emptied bins. Lucy Olofinjana from the Evangelical Alliance reports:

> Southampton City Council adopted a vision statement that the place would be 'good to grow up in and good to grow old in'. The churches of the city are committed to working together, partnering with the council and helping it prosper once again – to see the vision become reality. Southampton Christian Network is made of churches and para-church organisations who pray for the city. Paul Webber from Above Bar Church said: 'We are about 40 leaders meeting for a termly Saturday morning breakfast, a monthly Esther Prayer meeting and regional prayer meetings around the city.'
>
> To serve the city more effectively, the Southampton Christian Network, the Churches Together group and the Southampton Pastors

Network (mainly Black Majority churches) came together to form Love Southampton. In the light of the cuts – £25 million and 300 jobs to go in one year alone – the council asked for the help of the churches. The council had set out four areas of particular need; youth unemployment, youth clubs, childcare provision and a shortfall of families willing to foster and adopt vulnerable children.

A meeting responding to the cuts was held for church and community leaders and attended by around 400 people. 'We saw this as a significant opportunity for the Church to respond and the potential to make an impact,' explained Paul Woodman, leader of City Life Church. Churches realised that between them there were 17 paid youth workers and 37 mother and toddler groups – the resources and the opportunity to serve the wider community. Several working groups were formed to explore ways to address particular areas: open access youth provision, work with under-fives, fostering and adoption, post-16 housing and hardship.

'We all committed to 21 days of prayer and then we got practical,' continued Paul. 'We've managed to keep youth services open that were to close, youth drop-in centres are open for more sessions and we've increased output and help for families. Churches are more engaged and the city council has saved a lot of money. I have built stronger personal links with other church leaders when working together in niche and practical ways, like looking hard to find foster carers, rather than planning a basic church event. United for purpose.'

As churches have demonstrated that they can deliver successful initiatives, there is greater credibility, increasing partnership and a broader conversation about involvement. Street Pastors has had a strong presence for more than four years and there are five Healing on the Streets (HOTS) teams working in different suburbs of the city. Other projects include a pregnancy counselling service, 'messy church' on local estates and four food and one clothes provision outlets. Each week there are co-ordinated meals for homeless or individuals who are struggling financially. Peter Lambros from Portswood church said: 'We provide free breakfast each Saturday for around 60 people but it's not just about food, it's about friendships, offering a safe place and a listening ear. Working together we are more effective – like a fishing net instead of individual rods.'

Christians have also been very involved with establishing the two new Oasis Academies which replaced four old schools under threat of closure. Churches are collaborating together across the city to ensure sufficient schools work, assemblies and RE lessons. Together with New Generation Schools Trust, local churches have applied to open a new primary free school, Hope Community School, in the city centre.

Local government spent £1.2 million a year paying agencies to search for families able to provide a home for vulnerable children in need of foster care or adoption. Through establishing Families for Forty, churches committed to find the council more foster carers. Since March 2013 more than 70 people have applied to become foster carers. The Alliance's Home for Good initiative, learning from the success of Southampton, is now working with churches across the UK to achieve the same.

One strategic way to understand better what the churches of a town or city provide for its residents is to carry out a faith audit survey. This asks key questions about the services each church provides to the community and then is able to quantify those results in presentations to the council or other services and begin a fruitful conversation. Faith audit surveys were first carried out in Stoke, led by Lloyd Cooke who heads Saltbox, the charity that delivered, coordinated and encouraged social action across the city. Chester was the second city to undertake this innovative approach. Andy Glover reflects:

In 2009/2010, Link Up undertook a full audit of the faith sector across the Cheshire West and Chester area. Based on the work and methodology of the Saltbox Christian Centre in Stoke-on-Trent and Staffordshire, a report was produced in late 2010. The findings of this audit gave a 'snapshot' of West Cheshire's Faith Sector across all faiths, all communities and all projects and with this information we have developed a strong and fairly unique working relationship with the local authority.

Out of the developing relationship with CWaC and in recognition of the outcomes from the 2010 Faith Audit – Link Up has set up a new project called 'Standing in the Gap'. Building on some funding it received in 2012 together with the funding support of local churches, Link Up was able to employ two part-time staff: an administrator for Link Up (two days) and the project manager for [the] Standing in the Gap project. The Standing in the Gap project started in April 2013 and was a three-year project. One of its main goals was to carry out a second Faith Action Audit across the borough to see how the landscape of community action had changed since 2010. Link Up became the 'one stop shop for faith' sector in Cheshire West.

The Cinnamon Network led by Matt Bird working with Lloyd Cooke very helpfully enabled other cities and towns to carry out their own surveys which produced some very good results in building relationships with local authorities.

Siân Wade from Lincoln describes its effect:

Many years Lincoln has been a city that has been off the beaten track. It has a population of 100,000 people, a stunning cathedral, two universities and a heap of great forward-thinking churches. There had always been a sense of the need to work better together as churches across the city and a few partnerships had been made to bring new projects into the city, but we were all still too busy in our own little corners doing our own thing.

In 2015, we joined with the Cinnamon Network and did an audit across the city to discover how much social action was done by faith groups, and the results were incredible. It made us stop in our tracks and realise that although we were all working hard at serving our local communities we could really work better if we did some joined-up thinking. This was emphasised at our celebration event in the cathedral where the leader of our city council, armed with the results of the audit, asked why churches didn't work better together in order to partner with the council as one voice.

So Lincoln Active Faith Network was born. It had been an idea for a few years, but we felt that there was now a window of opportunity to run with it. The steering group is made up of people from all different denominations with one desire: to bring unity to the churches across the city. We have church leaders meeting once a month to pray for each other and pray for our city, with an annual joint prayer meeting every January for all churches. We have a new online system being created to pull together all the resources and projects that each church offers in order to see people's needs are met and to engage them with their local churches. We are having discussions with the local council about creating a covenant between Lincoln Active Faith Network and the local council to seal this new working relationship and provide the basis of a two-way partnership.

We recently met as a group of forty church leaders and Christian workers to listen to Ian Mayer share the journey of a unity movement in Doncaster, and to be inspired by what could be. There was a real sense of anticipation and togetherness. We may not lead church in the same way or agree on everything, but we do have two main things in common: we love Jesus and we love Lincoln.

We want to see our city restored spiritually and practically. Doing nothing is not an option and we believe, with God on our side, our city has a great future in store!

This same story is repeated in Sunderland, one of our newest unity expressions led by Deb Fozzard, who informs us:

The Sunderland Faith Audit was to be the first major undertaking for the newly formed Sunderland Connect Network. Whether it was to gather statistics or find out what is being done in the city, all agreed that it created a great opportunity to contact churches and assess just what impact the Church was having on Sunderland. The results were fascinating and actually showed that the Church is very much alive in the city and doing a great work.

We are now seeking to build upon the information we have. Through the Network we can create a central link for the Christian community and local authority. This will create an opportunity for greater impact – one thing we have learned over the years is that when people with a similar heart and different skills, talents and gifts come together so much more can be achieved than one person working on their own. We want as a network to help facilitate that coming together.

The audit has highlighted that 74 per cent of the projects being run by churches and faith groups are done in partnership with other organisations. 74 per cent of those that responded said they wanted a closer relationship with other organisations.

We are already working alongside a group of church leaders who regularly pray for the city and we are looking to encourage more interaction with each other as well as those representing the various organisations.

Doing social action projects, like those highlighted in the faith audit, is important, but what is most important are the reasons why we do them and this is the heart of Sunderland Connect Network. We have a hope for our city and that is to see lives transformed: we believe ultimately it is God who does this but we also need to play our part. We want the people of Sunderland to associate 'church' with being a good thing – outward-looking, relevant, a place of safety, support and community but most importantly a place of hope.

The stories of joined-up social engagement across cities and towns are now so numerous that this is just a snapshot of what God is doing through His body. This is a significant game-changer in what the Church does and how it is perceived.

In Bath they are actively working in partnership with civic authorities. Sir Peter Heywood, one of the leaders, describes it:

> now we have very close relationships with the local council. Every year we jointly host a conference, bringing together Church and civic leaders. In 2016 our keynote speaker was the Archbishop of

Canterbury. Our discussions with the council have led to the establishment of a local Home for Good movement to encourage adoption and fostering in the local Christian community. We are now actively engaged in conversations about the management of local children's and youth centres.

In Basingstoke, the borough council recently asked the churches to set up a winter night shelter of the pop-up variety, ie various town centre churches each opened their doors one night a week. More than 260 volunteers came forward and were trained to support this initiative. The project was such a success that at the end of the winter, the council put on a thank-you event with more than 200 public figures, volunteers and a few shelter guests attending.

Across Reading through the ministry of RCN, an incredible amount of service has been taking place over many years. Alan Magnuson, one of the key leaders, gave us an overview:

> In 2008 a few leaders of RCN caught the vision of Street Pastors and the initiative was launched in February 2009.
>
> We are usually on patrol from 10pm to 3am every Friday and Saturday night to care, listen and help people in the Reading town centre.
>
> We were invited to patrol inside Reading Festival and since then we have been invited back each year, and this year we had a tent at the festival. We have also been invited by the police to have extra patrols during Freshers' Week at the university. Further

doors have opened for us to cover Henley Festival and provide Rail Pastors at local train stations where there has been a high risk of suicides taking place.

The FIRST Stop project grew out of Street Pastors: originally this was a bus that was set up near the main area of clubs in the town centre to relieve some of the pressure on A&E at the Royal Berks Hospital at weekend night-times. In recent months this concept has moved from a bus in the centre of town to Reading Minster church in St Mary's Butts. People who require first aid, information, refuge, safety or medical treatment on a Friday or Saturday night between 9pm and 3.30am can head there from being in town. FIRST Stop works closely with Street Pastors and it's great to have this based in Reading Minster church.

During autumn 2013, RCN invited a series of guests to the leaders' prayer gathering who came to talk about the growing crisis facing social services in most towns and cities across the UK. This is a crisis affecting increasing numbers of children and young people who need long-term foster carers ... who are simply not available. We listened to people who could tell us about the current needs in Reading. We then heard a very exciting story emerging from Southampton Christian Network, where the churches have embraced a vision together to find families for forty children and young people.

Home for Good: Reading was set up to find fifty families over a three-year period to care for children through fostering or adoption. We believe that it is God's heart that Christians should step forward and offer their homes and families as places to care for vulnerable children, and that churches in Reading are able to offer love, fellowship and vital support to those who care for children.

Many of the examples above demonstrate how we work in partnership with a wide range of civic and other voluntary sector services. In 2011, through dialogue with key staff at the council we set up a strategic conference called Unlocking Opportunities to outline the needs facing the town in the areas of Adult Social Care and Housing. Over seventy church and social action leaders, as well as council representatives, came together to discuss how the Church might be a part of the solution to some of these needs.

As a direct result of this conference and the subsequent follow-up, we set up Engage Befriending, which is a home visiting/befriending initiative for older people living in Reading borough. This was modelled on and implemented by the person who had set up the Link Visiting Scheme in neighbouring Wokingham, which has been running for many years. Volunteers each visit one person who would like a befriender to visit them in their home. This could be due to ill health, disability, or other reasons leading to isolation or loneliness.

Following the financial crash of 2008 and the subsequent fallout, which is still working through the system in terms of drastic cuts to local services, we have seen a significant increase in rough sleeping and homelessness in Reading.

As a response to this we have set up a winter months only night shelter run by local churches and led by Faith Christian Group, one of our long-established local Christian charities, who also run the local food bank among other projects.

The scheme uses a rota of seven local churches, each providing a team of volunteers for one night per week each over a period of a month, two months or three months.

This scheme has been widely praised by all those involved including St Mungos, who are commissioned by Reading Borough Council to run outreach services to those on the streets. And to cap it all ... a number of the guests not only found themselves a bed for the night but were able to be housed more permanently ... and even get a job.

In Doncaster, a host of services are provided by the churches all linking together in One Heart One Voice, including debt advice through Christians Against Poverty (CAP), Street Pastors, food banks, Teen Challenge, civic forums and summits, meetings with elected members, Home for Good fostering support and missional business lunches.

The refugee crisis affecting the Middle East and Europe has led a number of city-based unity movements to respond. Churches Together in South London (CTSL) in response launched a new campaign called London United. This encourages churches of all denominations to showcase their community work, particularly for refugees, asylum seekers and destitute migrants. Throughout the Christmas season, people can share stories of community cohesion in the capital, using the hashtag #LondonUnited. CTSL represents more than fifty local ecumenical networks across ten London boroughs south of the River Thames. CTSL's main events have focused on the refugee response and it is clear that the Church's joint efforts to welcome people who have been forced to move has been a driving force in unity.

The Croydon churches responded very quickly to a refugee crisis that hit their town recently. Reuben Martin, one of the leaders, details for us the situation and how they responded to it:

> The Domesday Book of 1086 says these words about Croydon: 'In Croydon there is a church'. And in 2016 the Church in Croydon uses these words to work together in unity so that together we can build the kingdom of Jesus in Croydon.
>
> This autumn, we had the chance to do that, together. In the centre of Croydon is a building called Lunar House – the immigration centre for the whole of the United Kingdom. On a Friday evening in October, the British government announced that the following week hundreds of refugee children were being brought to Britain from the 'Jungle' refugee camp in Calais, France – brought to Britain thanks to the Dublin 3 accord and Dubs Amendment to the Immigration Act.
>
> These children were due to be brought to Croydon. Immediately, the Croydon Church responded, from Catholics to Pentecostals, from Baptists to Anglicans, from Quakers to new churches, joining the civic society group Citizens UK to

welcome these children to Britain. Each day as the coach arrived, the Croydon Church welcomed these refugee children with banners, balloons, cheering and applause. Inside Lunar House, the Croydon Church acted as responsible adults for the children as they were interviewed by Home Office staff. Some of the kids described their time in the Jungle as a 'living hell', but then described the welcome they received by the Croydon Church that week as 'the first time they'd felt loved in ages'.

In Croydon, we've worked hard at church unity – that's why when the call came to be the hands and feet of Jesus we were able to move quickly to go build the kingdom of Jesus in Croydon by helping putting a smile on the faces of these refugee kids.

Cultural transformation

One popular definition regarding culture is 'this is how we do things around here'.

This definition is particularly relevant to understanding our places and nation. Each country has its own specific cultural norms, attitudes and behaviours and each place within that country is unique. For the past seven years my wife, Lesley, and I have lived on a social housing estate in Wythenshawe, one of the poorest parts of Greater Manchester; however, for most our ministry we lived and ministered in Altrincham, only three miles away, which is one of the most affluent areas in Greater Manchester. The two places may be extremely close geographically but the cultures are not. How we do things in Wythenshawe is a million miles away from how people did things in

Altrincham. Cultural transformation is not about making Wythenshawe more like Altrincham, because both cultures have their beauty and ugliness. And affluence certainly doesn't make for greater closeness to the kingdom of God. Cultural transformation is about each unique culture flourishing and reaching its full potential; as no one human being is the same, so is no one community. How the values and norms of the kingdom of God, such as love, justice and truth, are expressed in any place will be beautifully different and yet similar. The coming kingdom of God is arriving in both and any culture to challenge, expose and defeat the social norms and values that create poverty, injustice, relationship breakdown, abuse of power, murder, greed, dishonesty and much more beside.

The role of the whole body of Christ across a city or town is firstly to open up its own church cultures to be transformed, to become more 'Christian', to be the shining example of that coming kingdom and to join God in His cultural transformational work. So as our own 'ways of doing things around here' are being shaped, challenged and changed, we go out into our places of work, the spheres of culture and neighbourhoods to join Christ in His kingdom work. If Christ, as Kuyper says, declares everything as 'Mine', then He will repossess all things; from the Church to the hospital, from the police station to the school, every culture and subculture, every institution and sphere is, and will be, affected by the norms and values of the kingdom of God. Our role as followers of this coming King is to be His body, His arms, mouth and feet into culture. To speak and act in kingdom ways, to effect change in vision and strategy, in HR and sales, in medical procedures and educational development and much, much more besides.

This big vision for the cultural change of places can only ever really be realised if the Church operates as one body, not only affecting culture from the institutional local church perspective but as God's people in education, arts, business, health, politics, family life, neighbourhoods, sports, social services, etc. The work of the London Institute of Contemporary Christianity (LICC) and others in encouraging Christians to identify their 'frontline' of service and possible effect for the kingdom has been vital in shifting us out of a perspective centred on local churches.

The next development we are identifying is the building of unity movements of ordinary lay Christians. In the same way that God has been drawing together church leaders in relation, prayerful and missional unity, He is, we believe, now drawing Christians in education, arts, business and other spheres to collaborate in the kingdom vision for cultural change. As with the church leaders, this must be interdenominational to effect the most change.

In Bristol, responding to the focus of an initiative called Forum for Change led by Marijke Hoek from the Evangelical Alliance, they have begun to set up networks of Christians in the cultural spheres across their city over the last few years. Under the leadership of Together4Bristol, involving some key leaders such as Roger Allen and Dr Sheena Tranter and others, they now have eight networks across the spheres of sports, arts, business and workplace, family, health, media, politics and social action, education and young people. Each sphere is led by core groups of Christians in those spheres whose role it is to enable, encourage, gather and be more strategically aligned to begin to see cultural change happen. As Roger Allen says, 'We long to see every sphere of life lived with Justice, Compassion and Humility made possible by a growing number of Christians, from every age-group, tradition, and culture: serving together, sharing the good news of Jesus and inspiring others to transform the whole of life in the region for good.'

They have written a creative newspaper article for the future that could be read in 2020 about the work of the churches in Bristol; it gives a flavour of their imagination and ambition.

A Big Vision for a Good Bristol 2020 (*The Post*, 31st December 2020)

Something remarkable has happened across Bristol in these last five years or so, which has helped to transform the Christian community and Bristol society and to 'make goodness fashionable' again. Under the banner, Together4Bristol (T4B), a 'unity for mission movement' has reached maturity as a 'network of networks', using a visionary, relational approach, with light structures.

Church leaders and Christian leaders from the prayer networks and spheres of society (Sport, Health, Education and Young People, Family, Politics and Social Action, Arts, Media and Business and Workplace) have regularly gathered together, building relationships and unity. The facilitators of the different spheres of life have formed core teams and had several wider gatherings, including conferences for hundreds of people.

They have also improved communication across the Christian community, including through websites and other social media.

They have worked together and have engaged with people of goodwill: to see people becoming followers of Jesus and every aspect of society in the region changed for good.

Everyday Christians, from all denominations, streams, class and ethnic backgrounds, have been praying in scores of small groups in churches, homes and workplaces across the Bristol region. Many Christian Workplace Groups have been set up, in schools, businesses, the BBC and hospitals. Nearly every church is linking with a local school.

Churches have become more city-focused. They have worked together to establish food banks, Street Pastors and debt advice centres. Christians have led the way. They have set up networks to work together strategically, to help ex-offenders and addicts. They are also leading three big investment funds for social enterprise.

They have had dozens of gatherings in open spaces (such as Parties in the Park) to engage with their local communities. Churches have helped to bring sports coaching to schools, especially in South Bristol. Over a couple of hundred children a year have made a commitment to Jesus at holiday sport camps. These and other activities, such as parenting courses, have helped local churches connect with a much broader cross section of society. The whole

Church had a whole year of mission to engage with people across the whole region.

They developed a learning hub to help change the mind-set of the Christian community, to release everyday Christians to be witnesses in ALL aspects of life.

The Christian community has learnt more about how to share their faith with people in word and deed in every aspect of life. Thousands of people have found that Jesus loves them. Their individual lives and families have been transformed as they learn to live God's way in every area of their lives and this has affected the whole region for good.

This vision statement is well under way, many of the goals in Bristol have already been achieved, and some surprising outcomes have taken place. A number of years ago, a young man with a passion for politics called Marvin Rees joined the politics and social action sphere; he was inspired, encouraged and supported by the group. They began to pray into the future of the city and two years ago he decided to stand for the post of elected mayor. This led to him being selected as the Labour party candidate and in June 2016 he was voted in to serve as the Mayor of Bristol. Change is happening, the kingdom of God is advancing and God's people are being strategic and coordinated.

This missional perspective of cultural transformation through unity is beginning to take root in other towns and cities as well. Christians Across Watford (CAW) have begun a Sports Network to engage with athletes and encourage outreach in the sporting sphere. Tim Roberts from Watford says:

We are collaborating with national and regional ministries like Christians in Sport and Kick London to see our work among the large sporting community in Watford grow and bring transformation. A church leader in one of our unity groups (prayer triplets) shared a vision he had to reach people in the sporting community, not least on Sundays by rearranging their church day. As an ex-footballer he said he had a heart to encourage trainee/professional footballers who are Christian. Another leader in that unity group shared about a young man in his church who was on the books with a local club, and facing challenges to work out his faith in that context. This conversation led to times of prayer, dreaming, a number of meetings with Christians in football, including some professional footballers and coaches, and interaction with national ministries.

A vision was presented to the Christians Across Watford members during the January 2017 'Looking Forward' residential, and subsequently to others within CAW. The result is the emergence of the CAW Sports Network and already a couple of 'Team Talk' events have been held to welcome Christian sportspeople from across the town's churches. Training, support networks, dance- and sports-based youth academies and outreach events are in the pipeline and a long-ignored sphere of town life can be impacted in new ways.

Alan Magnuson from RCN reflects on the challenges and success of setting up these groups and developing sphere networks across the area.

Finding, developing and supporting key leaders in each of the spheres of life beyond church and social action is an ongoing challenge. Various attempts have been made over the years to encourage and establish vibrant sphere-based networks, but it has proved difficult to see this become a growing reality. A number of people from the world of business have been operating under the banner of Reading at Work, seeking to encourage those called to outwork their faith in a wide range of employment situations.

A one-off event was held several years ago to try to re-energise this sphere, and there was some frank admission of the failings of both Church and business workers to understand fully each other's worlds and the pressures they bring. More recently there have been some signs of stirring in the area of the arts, with a few influencers coming together to share heart and vision, but this has not yet grown into a fully fledged and vibrant network.

Over the course of several years we worked closely with then local MP Martin Salter and his successful efforts to introduce legislation in 2008 to ban extreme internet pornography. This came about following the brutal murder of Jane Longhurst, whose killer had accessed such material and it was acknowledged as a significant influence on his behaviour. Jane's mother Liz lives locally, and she was a tireless campaigner for justice for her daughter and for the proposed change in legislation. RCN worked closely with both Martin and Liz and financially supported the campaign over a number of years until its successful conclusion.

Doncaster has approached the challenge of cultural transformation of the spheres of life by strategically focusing on four approaches across the city. Ian Mayer from One Heart One Voice explains:

Yes, unity works, and those outside of the Church are seeking it! Mission Doncaster has worked specifically within what we have termed the 'leadership quarters'. These groups are Church, commercial, civic and community. Each of these leadership quarters contributes to influencing people and places.

Church: This group includes those who are part of the Christian Church, including those who are involved in any form of Christian ministry or Christian charity. It can include church ministers, church officials, heads of Christian ministry or anyone who works or volunteers within the Christian Church.

Commercial: This group includes those who are involved in any form of business, or profit-making corporation. It can include business owners as well as business directors, managers, small business owners, entrepreneurs etc.

Civic: This group includes those who are involved in the statutory governance of a place. It can include elected officers, politicians, law enforcement and councillors, as well those who are employed by the local authority or work within other statutory bodies.

Community: This group includes those who work and volunteer within the local community. It can include residents' groups, heads of charities, health boards, social enterprises, councils for voluntary services, community action groups, non-Christian faith group leaders, leaders of societies or pressure groups etc.

There is overlap here, and we are not concerned with 'ring-fencing' any particular area. Overlap and interfacing is good. The lens through which we view a city is crucial to transformation. The leadership quarters within a city are the gateways to influence and the keys to strategic (and sustainable) change. If we are to have the biggest impact in our place, we need to ensure that we focus on the areas where the shape of our place is being formed, and the narrative is being written. Developing a portfolio of activities that grow leaders in these quarters and connect leaders in these quarters, is the key to influence.

Across London an imaginative unified approach to cultural transformation occurred from 2008 to 2012 in the area of the arts called the Pentecost Festival. Its originator and leader Andy Frost (Share Jesus) describes the scope and ambition of the project.

Many said it couldn't be done. London is more like a country than a city with a bustling 9 million residents living across thirty-three disparate boroughs. London is one of the most expensive cities on earth, with a thriving mainstream cultural and arts scene. And the Church in London is as diverse as the population it represents, often divided on grounds of theology, culture and style.

And yet, the vision we felt God was leading us into was a massive cultural and arts festival that took the Church outside of the confines of its building and put the Christian festival of Pentecost back on the map. Most of the events would be free and it would bring together the broad spectrum of churches across the capital together in unison to celebrate Pentecost like never before.

Share Jesus is a relatively small charity and this vision was deemed impossible by many as it would need a whole swathe of Christian agencies and London churches to commit. And yet the vision was compelling enough. People could glimpse what was possible. And so agencies and churches invested finance. They lay down their brands. And we saw the beauty of partnership.

Pentecost Festival ran from 2008 to 2012 in the heart of London. We pulled it off, not only once but for five years running. Each year there was an average of 100 unique events utilising eighty-plus venues attracting 30,000 Londoners and tourists to discover what Pentecost is all about. The programme was broad; there were film premieres in Leicester Square, hip-hop performances in parks and open spaces, and biblical performances in West End theatres. There were comedy nights in swanky bars; prominent scientists talking faith in iniversity lecture halls, and young people campaigning for justice on the streets. There were worship events in large auditoriums, gospel choirs on the streets and prayer stations in Trafalgar Square.

Some 100,000 printed programmes were distributed via local churches inviting London to discover that the Church is more than Sunday mornings – the Church is God's people on a mission to bring hope to the world. And the festival captured the imagination of the press with interviews on Radio 4, listings in *Time Out* and a live broadcast on BBC One. It demonstrated the power of a united Church to speak into society.

Many have since asked, how did you pull this off?

For sure, we were riding on a wave of God's grace. In human terms, with little financial underwriting and a 'learn-on-the-job' mentality, it really was a miracle that we landed even one festival. Reflecting on what we achieved, there were some key factors that meant it became a reality. Firstly, there was a clear vision. There was clarity about what we wanted to achieve and what we believed the impact could be. Secondly, the whole festival was as relational as we could make it, with the core team investing time building relationships with pastors and key stakeholders. And thirdly, the festival was about diversity. We didn't want 100 homogenous events but gave space to each church to bring what they did to the party. Each event was run by a local church and their values and ethos could be showcased. In essence, we provided a framework and a banner for others to do what they do best.

Over the five years of running Pentecost Festival in London, we learned so much about the breath and diversity of the Church. We saw remarkable partnerships emerge between churches as they

144

united in mission, learning from one another. When your programme involves Latino Pentecostals holding musical productions and Methodists exploring climate change and renewable energy, you remember just how important diversity in approach is, if you want to reach a city.

Ultimately we saw how effective the festival concept can be. The Church often holds many meetings in our buildings that fail to attract the masses. A party with food, music and good conversation that is hosted by people from diverse ethnic and cultural backgrounds gets people's attention. People came to faith, people came back to church and people discovered that the Church is live and active in the twenty-first century.

In 2012, we packaged up our festival experiences into a festival guide and trained eighty church unity groups on this model of mission. Many of these festivals continue each year to this day.

The arts has also been one of the focuses across Greater Manchester over the last few years. Visual and creative artists have been meeting together for more than four years to pray and support each other and to dream for their city region. Artist and curator Lesley Sutton leads this sphere group, and supported by its members, began a major arts initiative across the city called PassionArt.

In my role as both pastor's wife and artist/curator I grew very aware of how much the two spheres of the arts and the Church have in common and yet how distant the gulf between them was, not just in our city but throughout our contemporary Western culture. I felt challenged prayerfully to begin to both uncover and recover the relationship that the Church and the art world had shared throughout history and so my journey with PassionArt began in 2012. We began with the dream to recover the season of Easter and Lent within the cultural calendar of our city of Manchester. The Passion narrative is one of the most celebrated subjects in Western art. From paintings and sculpture to prose and music, many writers, artists and composers have created, and continue to create, exciting translations of the story and its underlying themes. However, in recent years the festival of Lent and Easter has fallen away from many of our cities' celebrations, so our aim is to re-establish this through our growing cultural partnerships with the cultural institutions of the city.

Over the past few years we have curated a series of visual arts trails and exhibitions that link the Passion story and themes arising from the season of Lent to the reality of everyday life. We exhibit and commission art works that invite quiet reflection on the universal themes of transformation, grief and loss, love and kindness and our longing for hope and stillness in a fallen and aggressive world. All of the art works we show are accompanied by written meditations that encourage the public to make meaningful connections with their own lives. Themes such as betrayal, forgiveness, compassion, bereavement and the fear of death are part of the universal human experience, no matter what faith or cultural background we are rooted in. Partnering with significant city centre venues, we have been able to grow meaningful conversations about faith as a part of the ongoing cultural language of the city, positioning faith stories and experiences within the secular conversations about mindfulness and the power of art to encourage contemplative time out in busy lives.

In our 2016 trail called Be Still (see www.passionart.guide) our venues estimated that more than 10,000 people had participated. We exhibited high quality contemporary art works by internationally renowned artists, such as installation artist Julian Stair who installed his disturbing work of contemporary life-size ceramic funerary vessels entitled *Quietus Revisited* in Manchester Cathedral. A video work by Adam Buick was installed over the altar of St Ann's Church as a call to stillness in a busy city, depicting a large church bell tolling in a sea cave as the tides changed, accompanied by a meditation on the Angelus bell, an ancient call to prayer at dawn, midday and dusk. We commissioned new works and directed people towards art works within the city gallery's collection, working with the gallery and other host venues to run art meditations and reflective workshops during lunch hours and after hours' events.

A group of refugees who visited the trail commented, 'To engage not just with our spiritual "side" but indeed the spiritual beings we all are through this trail was incredibly special indeed. To be able to discuss why death is terrifying, why cancer doesn't override or devalue the entirety of our

147

humanity and how deep beauty can be seen within our brokenness – asylum seeker, refugee or not – cannot help but stir that "Other" longing within us all. To have the space to do this though is not a lifeline many of us regularly give ourselves the gift of. To do this in a group can feel very vulnerable due to the expense of opening up our humanity even further but the rewards of this gift are worth more than gold.'

After the recent tragic terror attack in the city we are now working with our partners to host Be Vulnerable, an art trail for Lent 2018 that will engage with the narrative of our place at this time, as we learn to embrace our vulnerability and find strength through coming together; all themes from the life of Christ and particularly reflective of the Lent and Easter story.

Below are some of Lesley's reflections following these successful projects as to the process and goal of cultural transformation:

How do we see and bring about the kingdom of God in our cities and towns, in Manchester, Stafford, Birmingham, Plymouth or London? In reality how well do we truly re-imagine our town or city to be as God intended? How do we 'change the world' and what do we mean by transformation?

Like many others working secularly I am constantly exploring ways to make sense of and integrate my faith into my work and my creative practice; of understanding and blessing the communities I serve within to encourage values that

I believe are at the heart of the prayer, 'Thy kingdom come ...'

I am concerned that too often I can jump ahead and use trendy phrases in my prayer, worship and mission statements without taking the time to listen, learn and really unpack what needs to happen on a day-to-day basis at the heart of our communities in order to bring about a kingdom of love, truth, beauty and goodness – ie heaven on earth. So, how do we practically shape the culture of our place? How does the Church extend beyond its walls in our secularist, multicultural, fast-moving society and take its place in shaping the way our communities think, feel and live out their everyday lives?

Over the past few decades, the pace of cultural change in cities across the globe has accelerated considerably. It is therefore essential that the 'gathered' Church both understands and takes its place at the centre of culture as agents of creative transformation as well as being messengers of truth and goodness. To see mission as a vision for the whole of our communities that all are involved in, not just those called to full-time Christian work or doing church mission projects – doctors and nurses to have a vision for health, teachers and educators to have a vision for the improvement of education in their place, for those working in business to share values that impact the way their companies function and grow, and those called to work in the arts and media to have a kingdom vision as to how to shape the stories that go out to the households and communities across our cities and nation to have wholesome kingdom values that bless our communities.

The eminent contemporary theologian Walter Brueggemann in his book *The Prophetic Imagination* writes:

> The task of the prophetic ministry is to nurture, nourish and evoke a consciousness and perception alternative to the consciousness and perception of the dominant culture around us.[11]

He suggests that our calling, as the community of God's people, is the re-formation of God's kingdom on earth, through the living out of an alternative community to that which is dominant in our present culture. He highlights how the God-given prophetic imagination of Moses sought to evoke an alternative consciousness within the Israelite nation to that of the Egyptian society which dominated their lifestyle. But firstly for them to be able to move forward to this way of seeing they first needed to see and understand the context and culture within which they lived. To critique the dominating culture of Egypt that was totally consumed with the desire for excess, to hoard in barns excessive amounts of grain so that the elite would always feel in control and not have to fear scarcity; to use the asylum seeker as slaves to create a bigger and stronger economy for the rich and elite of Egypt – to limit their resources so that they were trapped in to forever making bricks

---

[11] Walter Brueggemann, *The Prophetic Imagination* (Minneapolis, MN: Fortress Press, 1978, 2001), p13.

without ever having a day's rest, as the values of the culture were to accumulate excess rather than to believe in the abundance of a creator God. He explains that the Israelite people needed to understand the culture within which they lived and served in order to desire a new way of living and being. In the same way as in Ancient Egypt over 3,000 years ago, the ethos of consumerism, self-satisfaction and success has come to define our contemporary Western culture and [has] infiltrated the very essence of how we live, both within and without the Church, thereby suggesting that we too need to encourage a prophetic imagination like Moses to speak in our time.

With this understanding of the prophetic in mind, I have found the arts to have a really significant role to play in the critiquing of the dominating culture and values of our time and place and of the imagining of an alternative consciousness; to suggest new and reformed ways of thinking, living and being; of seeing the world through the eyes of a loving God and not just through the distorted lens of negativity and despair that tends to dominate our screens, our newspapers and our everyday perceptions of life. But this way of thinking is transferable to all the spheres, in business, politics, health, education, sport etc

If we want to communicate relevantly we must first understand our audience, the culture they inhabit and the way in which they see and understand the world. This is called the sociological imagination – to engage in social and cultural

151

criticism and moral argument; to make connections between the larger picture of the social history of society to the smaller picture of the story of particular individuals within it.

To understand your town's or city's history, its changing story, its development and its vision for the future, to understand the context of the time and place that we say we want to change and transform, then where must we go but to its museums and galleries, libraries and theatres? These public spaces enable us to view these ideas not just from our own limited perspective but from the viewpoint of others who are culturally different to us but who share the same space. We can listen to our city's music and drama, read the poetry, literature and observe the art works, public sculpture, the architecture, interior design that all reveal a material expression of the way people think and feel. We must look at the new art on the street, the ghetto culture, club culture; visit the spaces where stories from migrant communities are shared. We can read the latest literature on display in Waterstones, watch TV, films, etc, for all tell a story of what our society's values are, what we believe in and what our priorities are. They can reveal our fears, anger and bitterness but also offer vision and hope and ideals to work towards. For culture helps to shape the way a city thinks, feels and acts.

Postscript to spiritual, social and cultural transformation

Spiritual, social and cultural transformation can involve large events, major projects and organised strategic networks in the spheres across a city, but it is also ordinary and down to earth. The everyday work of God's people in everyday life will provide the vast majority of cultural, social mission across a city. When we see ourselves as God's missionaries, His change agents into everyday life, those with a frontline, we take our place in simply listing to the Spirit and responding.

Paul Keeble and his wife, Judith, have served in some of the country's most deprived areas for more than thirty years. Paul shares how important it is for us to do mission with and among our communities in simple and ordinary acts of the everyday, to embrace vulnerability and humility and walk alongside people, rather than only create projects and programmes that can sometimes give us power over our neighbours rather than release them. For Paul, city and town transformation comes about through low-visibility acts that we can all live out daily as well as the bigger missional activities we often engage in.

Yesterday my next-door neighbour fixed the leaky pipes under our kitchen sink. He was made redundant recently and his poor spoken English makes him quite underconfident when it comes to applying for another job. We knew he was a bit of a handyman so we asked him to come in and take a look at the puddle on our kitchen floor. With a bit of pointing and sign language he told me what parts to get, and then came back to fit them. It's a job I maybe could have done myself (my wife isn't so sure), but our antennae are out for opportunities to build relationships with those we share our street with, and particularly for chances to let them serve us. In the case of this family, we have helped them on several occasions, including when they arrived, going to welcome them and to explain the complex process of taking the bins out (each house has four different ones. Note we did not offer to do it for them, but showed them how they could do it themselves). He was obviously pleased at the opportunity to repay a favour, and my hope is that his self-esteem has gone up a notch.

What does this have to do with mission? The concept of the missio Dei – the constant activity of a loving God as a missionary seeking to deepen his relationship with His creation – (making the Church's task one of joining in) gives scope for a deeper, holistic form of mission. God's desire for people is *shalom* – health of mind, body, spirit and community – which will include a sense of well-being and self-esteem. This comes right down into the small, everyday things of normal life – like bins and leaks and many more. I call this 'mission-with' and it is rooted in being present alongside others and building relationships. Not so we can bestow blessings on our poor, lost neighbours, but so we can live alongside, get to know, learn from and be blessed by, as equals, and when it comes to dealing with issues we share a concern about – such as a problem with gang violence – as co-workers. A part of them getting to know us will be getting to know Jesus in us having an effect on our attitudes and reactions. We don't hide our faith, but we also don't push it. We try to show it in the day-to-day and most days life is just like anywhere else. Our community is a diverse one, but we all do mostly the same things: like the school run, cook meals, moan about the weather … and take the bins out.

'With' has been called 'the most important word in theology'.[12] It is the active part of that amazing title of Jesus, 'Emmanuel', meaning 'God with us'. It speaks of the incarnation of Jesus as the ultimate incomer. 'The Word became flesh and made his dwelling among us.'[13] And he sends us as the Father sent him, [14] to be with people. It's all about relationship. I am evangelical by background and we are big on the great commission. But it is preceded by the great commandment, which is surely the lens though which we should view our commission. The two parts of that commandment – on which everything else depends – to love God with all we are and our neighbour as ourselves, are actually of equal importance (like the old Double A-Side if anyone remembers the vinyl single records). The Greek word

---

[12] Samuel Wells, *A Nazareth Manifesto: Being with God* (Chichester: John Wiley & Sons, 2015), p231.

[13] John 1:14a. Or 'The Word became flesh and blood, and moved into the neighborhood.' Eugene Peterson, *The Message: The Bible in Contemporary Language* (Colorado Springs, CO: Navpress, 2004), p1444.

[14] John 20:21.

for neighbour simply means 'near', so next door, next desk, co-worker, teammate.

Mission is often seen as events or activities: acts of service for or taking a message to. Nothing wrong with events and activities, but by their nature they are episodic, one-sided in power terms and not conducive to forming loving, empowering and equal relationships. And as we have seen, mission is much bigger. Particularly in a multi-faith context, beginning with a mission-with approach, being among, sharing life, building relationship (making it an 'always on' model), can earn the right to some more overt form of action, though it should never be seen as a means to that end. Over our time in this neighbourhood we have seen some lovely changes: now there is far less vandalism, graffiti, on-street drunkenness, overt racism, and far more engaging with and watching out for each other. There is more to do, not least a fly-tipping issue, but overall *shalom*/well-being levels have increased, not just because we are here, but because others have also responded to a gradual shift in atmosphere. Many of our Muslim neighbours now know the difference between a Christian and a *Christian*. Some neighbours have even come to our church carol service.

Mission-with can work in any context containing neighbours ... so just about anywhere. In our particular case that context has been an inner-city neighbourhood in Manchester. This brings a whole other dimension to the 'who' we have been with, in that we have been following a calling to choose to live long-term in the sort of area most people, given a Lottery win, aspire to move away from. This has been the classroom where mission-with has been/is being learned through being, doing and reflecting.

So that those relationships with neighbours can grow, where Christians are is of vital importance, and that in two senses. The first is summed up beautifully in a cartoon by Dave Walker at the front of my book, *Mission With*.[15] Titled 'Where the church is', it is a busy city scene with numerous arrows and the word 'here' pointing to a pedestrian, a bus passenger, a car driver, a shop assistant, a window cleaner and more. It is saying church is the people where they are and what they are doing and who they are with on the other six and a half days of the week when they are not warming a pew.

The second sense of 'where' is to do with where we choose to live. Surely, if our faith is more than a 'devotional add-on' to normal life, the big decisions are to be made by calling over comfort. Part of what led us to the inner-city over thirty years ago was seeing the imbalance between where most people lived and most Christians lived. If all Christians are actually living – or working – where God has 'placed' them, given the proportion in the inner city, that would seem to be a massive contradiction to God's 'preference' for the poor.

The New Testament letters contain next to no exhortation or how-to instruction to evangelise. But there is a lot about relationships: with God, with each other and with those outside of the Church – our

---

[15] Watford: Instant Apostle, 2017.

neighbours. Peter says: 'Always be ready to answer everyone who asks you to explain about the hope you have.'[16] Surely that is about an observed lifestyle causing curiosity. Half of the recorded words Jesus spoke were in response to questions related to His actions. I would now query an isolated outreach initiative such as litter-picking where a church visits and does something for a community. Being with people, encouraging picking up the litter together is better on several levels. But it is also harder and takes longer.

'We need to do our work and live our lives in a way that calls attention to the new Spirit that lives within us and who is changing us. We need to relate to people … in ways that create a sense of wonder. We must seek a spirituality that makes our lives eloquent.'[17]

This is city transformation from the low-visibility, micro end of the scale (see also mustard seeds, yeast), and it is one person and one leaky pipe repair at a time.

---

[16] 1 Peter 3:15, NCV.

[17] Bryant Myers, *Walking with the Poor: Principles and Practices of Transformational Development* (Maryknoll, NY: Orbis, 2000), p321.

Chapter 6
Old Words for a New Day

The call to love each other, to love God and the places we live in, is deeply rooted in the Bible. Below are some reflections on three key passages that help shape how we are to approach this calling and the implications it has for us.

The gathering in

He made known to us the mystery of his will according to his good pleasure, which he purposed in Christ, to be put into effect when the times reach their fulfilment – to bring unity to all things in heaven and on earth under Christ.
Ephesians 1:9-10

His intent was that now, through the church, the manifold wisdom of God should be made known to the rulers and authorities in the heavenly realms.
Ephesians 3:10

The existence and nature of the Church is very unusual in today's Western world, a place that has within it children and elderly people, teenagers mixing with people old enough to be their parents, the rich alongside the poor, the employed and unemployed, with women and men joining with those from many different nations and ethnicity.

Where else does this happen in our culture? A major event, perhaps, or a sporting occasion, but this isn't just for a one-off meeting but involves people who journey together for many years. How did this happen? Why do we do this? The Church gathers across this nation because we are deeply influenced by a God whose nature it is to gather together all of creation.

The Christian Faith has no knowledge of an isolated, private and disinterested God. The God of the Bible is a relational being, who exists as three persons gathered together as one being. He is a God who creates a world and human beings in order to live with Him, to be encircled by Him and loved. The arms of God are wide and encompassing around all He has made.

The world we live in, however, is often far from cohesive, with its struggles to maintain relationships and create loving and just societies. Instead of community we are often fragmented; instead of a cohesive society we are at odds with each other. So we fight our wars and hate our neighbours, we break covenants with marriage partners and wound our children. We look after ourselves and ignore the most vulnerable.

I used to minister in a very affluent area where the goal of life was to have a large house with a long driveway with electric gates to keep everyone as far away as possible. It was hard to have a conversation in that culture without being asked early in the proceedings about what job you had. This immediately placed you in a pecking order, either to distance you from those beneath you or perhaps to be advantageous to you when meeting someone above you. This society is a microcosm of the wider culture where we are increasingly becoming like water particles in space, floating around as separate molecules, having lost our cohesion and form.

And what is the response of God in this, the One whose encircling has been forced apart? Is it to push away in pain to defend Himself? No, it is one of grace as He reaches out to a universe in Christ Jesus and begins His plan of restoration by gathering together that which has been fragmented.

Ephesians chapter 1 says He has chosen us to be with Himself. We are not lost, we are being tracked down, we are being sought out. We are the sheep He is after, we are the coin He has lost, we are the son He is looking and waiting for to come home. His will and intent is 'to bring all things in heaven and earth together under one head, even Christ' (Ephesians 1:10, NIV 1984).

To 'gather together' is called in the Greek *anakephalaiosasthai*, which is more directly translated as 'gathering things together and presenting them as a whole'. This was used in Greek culture as adding up a column of figures and placing the total at the top. The word is used to describe at other points in the Bible, restoration, unity and the headship of Christ (Colossians 1:16, 20). Through sin, endless disorder and disintegration have come into the world, but in the end all things will be restored to their intended function and to their unity by being brought back to the obedience of Christ (Colossians 1:20).

'All things' includes secular and spiritual, any barriers of race or colour, culture, political and economic systems. That's the big plan. He's going to bring it all together again under Christ. He going to mend it, He's going to gather that which has been shattered and fragmented and bring it once again into His loving embrace. That's the picture of heaven to look forward to. A new world reconfigured, united, healed, restored, embraced. A safe place, a place of community and love, a place of deep relationships and healthy growth. A place of beauty without pollution and disease and injustice. A place of order and loving freedom.

The cosmos has been plunged into disintegration on account of sin and it is God's purpose to restore its original harmony in Christ. And how is He going to do it? This is the big shock, because He going to pilot it with one group of people. He is going to give the world a taste of what is to come, He is going to bring heaven on earth, and this is biggest shock of all – this great undertaking is called the *Church*.

'His intent was that now, through the church, the manifold wisdom of God should be made known to the rulers and authorities in the heavenly realms' (Ephesians 3:10). Ephesians is a big sermon on the eternal purposes of God, through Jesus, worked out in the Church. It's all about the mighty purposes of God for His Church. Paul sees its climax, the headship of Christ (Ephesians 1:22; Colossians 1:18, 24).

Paul prays for the Ephesian Church (Ephesians 3:14-19) that they might get hold of this truth. He prays for them to have their eyes opened to the purposes of God that they may have the faith to grasp the extent of the power of God to do this. He prays they may see the vision that He will bring about, that everything is brought together under Christ, the head of the Church. 'And God placed all things under his feet and appointed him to be head over everything for the church, which is his body, the fullness of him who fills everything in every way' (Ephesians 1:22-23).

So the Church is part of the final vision of all things. It's the trailer for the film! The Church is the fullness of God on earth. Where do you go to experience the abundance of God? Where do you go to touch eternity? To experience the love of another kind, the embrace of a God who is drawing you to Himself? You go to the Church! Jesus prays for the unity of His Church, that the glory in Him may be in His Church: 'Father, just as you are in me and I am in you. May they also be in us so that the world may believe that you have sent me' (John 17:21).

This is a very high view of Church ecclesiology, and a very high view of the mission of the Church. The people of God are drawn into the gathering arms of God, Father, Son and Holy Spirit. We do not just stand in the presence of God as individuals, we stand as the Church of God, embraced in His purposes. We are the body of Christ on earth and we carry out the gathering intentions of the gathering God.

1. We are the community that lives out the new cohesive society

Ephesians 2:13-15: 'now in Christ Jesus you who once were far away have been brought near by the blood of Christ … he … has destroyed the barrier, the dividing wall of hostility … making peace.' So Ephesians goes on to explain to us about this new society, this joined together community. The major reconciliation/unity is, of course, between Greek (Gentile) and Jew who are no longer strangers but fellow citizens (Ephesians 2:19).

The writer gives practical ways this can be lived out where we are encouraged to live a new way with each other in patience, humility and gentleness. We are to work for unity, not fragmentation: 'Make every effort to keep the unity of the Spirit through the bond of peace' (Ephesians 4:3). We are to be honest, not to let anger burn us up, to never take what isn't ours, and to watch our mouths, to not slander or be malicious; to be kind and compassionate with each other (Ephesians 4:25-29). We are implored to have no hint of sexual immorality, which fragments relationships (Ephesians 5:3), and to submit to one another in a new order of relationships (Ephesians 5:21). Our relationships are not to be based on confrontation and power but on love and submission. A new order is to be lived out here, in marriage, in home life, in business life. No divisions, no favourites, no racism, sexism or ageism.

That's what unity is all about; we are to display the gospel of the gathering God; we witness to Him in our lives together. We are the evidence of the glory of God on earth, and in His power we can live differently. The master plan of God for bringing unity and peace in place of hostility and estrangement had been put into effect in Christ, and His Church was to be the reconciling centre for this. In the Church, all divisive forces can be neutralised and an all-inclusive fellowship can be established; this is proof of the 'manifold wisdom' of God.

2. We are a display to the heavenly realms that God brings things together, not to be uniform and boring but to be beautifully diverse

'His intent was that now, through the church, the *manifold wisdom* of God should be made known to the rulers and authorities in the heavenly realms' (Ephesians 3:10, my italics). 'Manifold wisdom of God' is a very interesting word in the Greek; it is *polupoikilos*, which is used in classical Greek writing with reference to cloth or flowers, describing the intricate beauty of an embroidered pattern or the endless variety of colours in flowers. Its meaning is that in God there is the expression of a richly diversified and many-splendoured truth. The pure light of God refracted through the prism of the material creation breaks into all the colours of the spectrum. That's the wisdom of the Church, declared in Christ!

So God takes the irreconcilable, the diverse cultures, backgrounds, classes and nations and makes them one and still retains their uniqueness. The principalities and powers are about division, strife, enmity. Their values? Uniformity, control and fear.

But a new wisdom is declared to them and to the world, that love brings us together and love brings out the very best in us all. So the young and old stand together, alongside the rich and poor and the black and white.

Chinese people are joined with South American Indians and former terrorists are reconciled to the police. A former abuser is gathered together with their healed victim in forgiveness and reconciliation and the Pentecostal prays with an Anglican and a Baptist builds friendship with a Catholic. This is the multifaceted, rainbow-coloured gathering in God.

3. We are the gathering arms of God as He works out His mission to gather all that has been lost

We don't just live in this community of the gathered, we are sent out to gather in as well. So we immerse ourselves in the fragments of society, not hiding behind our walls, but we live as Christ lived with the people among the lost in the world, so that, through the love of God, that which has been lost is found and brought into Christ.

It's a powerful thing when the Church that displays the many-splendoured diversity of the wisdom of God in Christ then becomes the hands and feet of that God as He seeks to reach out to the fragmented world. In this gathered-in unity, we reach out to the homeless, the vulnerable and the hurting; we declare and display the good news of Christ. In unity we take our spiritual responsibility over our towns and cities for Christ. We declare to the heavenly realms that Satan is bound, that injustice is defeated, that *shalom* will come.

If we just individualise this message to our own local church and don't have an expression of this message among the churches of our area, our witness to the gathering God is severely compromised. If we don't start thinking 'one Church, many congregations' across a town or a city, we will not display the manifold wisdom of God in Christ.

The gathering God has placed His arms of love around us, and we, in turn, with our arms around each other, reach out to gather all things together under Him.

The dripping beard

> How good and pleasant it is when God's people live together in unity!
> It is like precious oil poured on the head, running down on the beard, running down on Aaron's beard, down on the collar of his robe.
> It is as if the dew of Hermon were falling on Mount Zion.
> For there the LORD bestows his blessing, even life for evermore.
> *Psalm 133:1-3*

Walter Brueggemann, the Old Testament scholar, argues that the Psalms can be divided into three sections.[18] Firstly Psalms of Orientation, where life is good, full of blessing and joy and all it should be, and God is great, so we must give thanks. He then describes another section as Psalms of Disorientation, where life is awful, the writer is in fear for his life and not sure God is around. The third and final section consists of Psalms of Reorientation, where God has

---

[18] Walter Brueggeman, *Message of the Psalms: A Theological Commentary* (Augsburg Old Testament Studies (Minneapolis, MN: Fortress Press, 1985).

come and saved the writer out of the difficulties, and he is now safe and thankful.

According to Brueggemann, Psalm 133 is a Psalm of Orientation. Isn't it great when people live in harmony together; it's full of blessing! The writer was obviously having a good day. This is the world of good friends, happy families, social cohesion and great kindness. However, we know life isn't always like this: divorce happens, families break down and neighbours fall out. Loving, trusting relationships can be diminished by miscommunication, disloyalty and bitterness. Unity within the body of Christ isn't often as tranquil as depicted in Psalm 133. Church history is littered with stories of distrust, jealousy, apathy, ego, arrogance, fear and selfishness.

So is this psalm a utopian, unattainable dream? The context of this psalm is very interesting, since it was probably written at a time of great division in post-exilic times. The northern kingdom and southern kingdom were split apart. There was significant political disunity; the northerners based around Samaria and Mt Hermon were not seen as legitimate Jews, while the south had Jerusalem and Mt Zion. This political, religious and cultural split continued until Jesus' time, when we sense the tension in the meeting between him and the Samaritan woman by a well in John 4. This disunity is again exposed when He goes on to teach the parable of the Good Samaritan.

So why is the psalmist saying these things in the context of disharmony among God's people? Well, it depends on where you are standing. If your perspective is on earth, then this doesn't make sense, but if your perspective is in the heavens, and he is declaring the true heavenly reality of life, then perhaps it does.

This psalm is a statement of heavenly reality, a declaration of what really is and will be, a prophetic statement. He knows that deep in the fabric of life, there is a force that is so overwhelming that nothing will get in its way; a movement in this universe towards perfect harmony and unity of all things.

The psalm describes this in very interesting ways.

It's the very fabric of creation: This unity is described as 'precious' and 'good', which are the same terms used in Genesis chapter 1 to describe creation itself: 'And God saw that it was good' (Genesis 1:4, 10, 12, 18, 21, 25). The word 'good' can be translated as precious, unified and harmonious. The images of water and oil are also natural metaphors for God's presence in the New and Old Testament. So this unity is like a natural life force, like the sun rising, my body healing, and plants growing. Harmony is the stuff of Eden of creation itself. Unity here is not just a state of peace achieved between people, it's part of the fabric of the universe itself, it comes from God and is part of the nature of God.

It's overflowing and abundant: The oil is poured out and there is so much of it that it covers a grown man. The dew falls on Mt Hermon and several hundred miles away its effects are felt on Mt Zion. Mt Hermon is the life force over all of Israel: it's the source of all the fresh water across the nation and without it there would be no habitable land. This life force of unity brings with it fruitfulness, life and abundance and it can never run out or be drained.

It's a force coming to the world: This life force, this act of nature, this abundant life-giving water and oil is coming down from heaven towards us, it's flowing upon us, it's flowing around us like a river, it's falling down. This can't be stopped, it can't be avoided it, it will find us. It's a blessing that you're going to get even if you don't want it, it's the future projection of history.

The teaching of this psalm should not be a surprise to us as Christians. We find it a foundational teaching within the theology of the Trinity where God is a unity of three persons. The theme is taken up again in Genesis where in Eden unity is lived and then broken through the Fall. Humanity walks away from it and Cain kills Abel; relationships break down, and people don't live in unity, they don't care for and love others, they oppress and control and destroy, as Egypt did to Israel.

But this abundant, overwhelming life force still comes to us as God calls, and gathers in, creating Israel as His people to be a light on a hill, to live as a witness to the unifying God.

Jesus comes to those on the fringes, those left out, lost from the family, and He talks about the oil of forgiveness, the primacy of loving our neighbour and the need to be unified with God so we can be unified with each other. He prays His greatest prayer before His death, that they may be one, unified, in harmony, gathered together in Him. Then His Church is birthed and they display this unity, they hold things in common, they have no needy people among them, they serve the poorest and bring them in from the outside.

Jesus declares in John 17:23 that when His Church lives in unity the world will see that He has been sent by the Father. When the world experiences the love and sacrifice in the Church, they will automatically begin to see the life force behind that unity. A Church that dwells in unity is therefore to be celebrated in the heavenly places; it's very precious, it's like oil over your head, it's like water flowing down from the mountains in a parched land, it's like a place of blessing. We are standing right in the middle of a life force, a river of harmony, a place of blessing.

When the world sees strong friendships between people of different denominations, pastors honouring one another, seeing themselves not as independent and aloof but part of a city-wide team of clergy serving the city, Christians overflowing with love for the people of the area, their neighbours, their work colleagues, Christians with a vision of unity who are seeking for things to work better in the city, resulting in fewer people outside in poverty and marginalised, Christians with a vision for unity in civic life and family life, then they will know Jesus was sent by the Father. They will see the life force of God in this world and want to be part of it.

This psalm is an invitation to be part of this move of God. It's not a command, it's not an edict, it's not a criticism or dictate to get your life sorted out, it's an invitation to come and be part of this movement of God's unifying love.

So with the Holy Spirit, I look at my relationships and see if God's life-unifying force is working in me to make up with someone, forgive someone, make an effort with someone. Work with someone I find difficult. Love those around me. As a Church leader I am invited to take my

171

work for unity to another level of prayer, support and friendship with other leaders, helping, honouring, sharing resources for the sake of harmony and the area.

As a Christian in the workplace or local neighbourhood I am encouraged to build long-lasting friendships and supportive relationships that become life-giving for the hospital I serve in or the school I'm a part of. I'm to meet and pray with other Christians in those spheres of life to build movements for transformation that become part of the unity coming down from the heavenly places.

So as Christians we are invited to get in the middle of this harmony river, to go out to work for peace and harmony in the world, to embrace a vision of what will be in the future, and of the God who has it in His heart that this town or city will be more peaceful, integrated, less unequal, with fewer divisions, stronger families, fewer people on the margins, and more gentle.

This invitation also come to me personally. I'm invited into the loving, united relationship of the Trinity. I'm called to be at peace with God. I'm to experience the falling down of the oil on my head and the water of His Spirit on me, the feeling of coming home to the Father.

Once we are part of this life-giving, abundant, unifying movement from heaven to earth, we then begin to stand in the flooding of God's blessing and life. Then we are able to bless the places God has placed us within, and we in turn are blessed and begin to prosper (Jeremiah 29:4-7).

The King's Dome

(by Stephen Sutton, a unity leader in Middlesborough)

> This is what the LORD Almighty, the God of Israel, says to all those I carried into exile from Jerusalem to Babylon: 'Build houses and settle down; plant gardens and eat what they produce. Marry and have sons and daughters; find wives for your sons and give your daughters in marriage, so that they too may have sons and daughters. Increase in number there; do not decrease. Also, seek the peace and prosperity of the city to which I have carried you into exile. Pray to the LORD for it, because if it prospers, you too will prosper.'
> *Jeremiah 29:4-7*

The year is 598 BC, Jerusalem, God's city, the centre of God's nation, the place where life is supposed to function and operate under God's rulership. The place that holds in the Ark of the Covenant the presence of Yahweh. That place has just been invaded by a foreign power. God's city is now occupied! The leaders of Jerusalem are ... in chains and are now slaves in the city of Babylon. The temple, the very dwelling place of the presence of God, has been raided and desecrated. Men, women and children have been murdered. The people of God are no longer in the city of God, they now find themselves as slaves, exiles, foreigners in the city of Babylon.

They sit by the rivers of Babylon, looking out to the southern horizon, weeping as they remembered Zion.

These are real people, hurt, displaced, battered, forgotten, forsaken. Now waking up to a new life, no longer in God's city, where God is supposed to rule … now they are in Babylon where it feels very, very clear … God does not rule.

And so what does God have to say to these people?

'Build houses and settle down; plant gardens and eat what they produce. Marry and have sons and daughters; find wives for your sons and give your daughters in marriage, so that they too may have sons and daughters. Increase in number there; do not decrease.'

Jeremiah 29:5-6

They must have felt like [shouting] out, 'What is God going on about? Don't talk about gardens and baby-making. Do You know where we are? Have You been watching what has been happening? We need salvation from Babylon, a victory over Babylon, we need a plague and revenge upon Babylon.'

But God responds in this passage, 'No, I am not busting you out, I want you here, you are in the place where you are because I want you there, so here's what I want you to do: go and unpack your bags, build houses, get yourself a garden going on, get married, raise your kids, in fact, while you're there, why don't you sort out wives and husbands for your kids? Because you're staying! I want you right where you are right now. I want you, My people, in the middle of this land here. My temple might not be here, this city might not bear My name. But I say to you, you are My

174

people, and you are called to be My people here in this land.'

So now they have got to figure out how they are going to do that! In this land. Not in Jerusalem. Not in the promised land of milk and honey, but in this land. In this city. Right here in the middle of Babylon. How are you going to be 'My people'?

So 'seek the peace and prosperity of the city to which I have carried you into exile. Pray to the Lord for it, because if it prospers, you too will prosper' [Jeremiah 29:7]. Seek its *shalom* and its prosperity. *Shalom* is a Hebrew word that we just can't fit into [an] English word. It has the feeling of peace, but also it describes a state of wholeness, completeness or harmony.

To understand the context of this passage we need to go back to Genesis chapter 1. In the beginning, when God made the world, what was it like? In the beginning it says it was good. Everything functioned in the way it was designed to function: there was order, creativity, work, relationship, harmony, there was harmony between God and people, harmony between people and people, harmony between people and the rest of creation. It was good and at peace, whole and complete; this was *shalom*. You see, *shalom* isn't just a word that means peace, *shalom* means everything being as God wants it to be. It's God's state of peace and wholeness and completeness.

And God says to these exiles in the middle of a tough city, a city full of violence, sin, corruption, brokenness, 'Seek the *shalom* of the city that I have carried you into.'

The Bible uses other words to describe this same concept; it just comes at it from a different angle. You might

175

be more familiar with the phrase, 'the kingdom of God'. Back in Genesis chapter 1 the world was described as good and that goodness [was] *shalom* because God was King. Everything is *shalom* when God is King.

But that state of God's kingdom and *shalom* in Genesis chapter 3 suddenly is broken apart. Humankind want to be their own kings, they want to do things their way and not God's way. So everything gets broken, *shalom* is not here anymore. God's kingdom is not here anymore. Instead of the kingdom of God on earth, we get a millions of mini-kingdoms of 'Me'.

However, when Jesus comes He declares that the kingdom of heaven has drawn near: 'Jesus went throughout Galilee, teaching in their synagogues, proclaiming the good news of the kingdom' [Matthew 4:23].

This is what He was about. This is what He was saying and showing people. God is becoming King again, this is what it looks like: the blind have sight, captives are set free, storms are stilled, sinners are forgiven, outcasts are made welcome. Everything changes.

What is the good news? What is the gospel of Jesus Christ? It's the good news that the kingdom of God is nearby. It's coming back again. God is becoming King again. Heaven on earth is becoming true again, *shalom* is being restored again.

This is a gospel of people being saved from their sins, but it's also about the entire cosmos, the earth, the land, the cities and towns we live in being saved from the power of sin, and death, and violence and chaos. Because when God becomes King, when *shalom* is restored, it doesn't just change our interior spiritual life, it changes everything.

Here is another way of understanding the kingdom of God. It's the King's dome. It's the dome in which God is King, under which everything happens by the King's will. So when I pray, 'Jesus be King over my life', I am stepping into a whole new way of life, I am stepping into a dome where Jesus gets His own way with me. Now that dome changes everything in my life. Not just my soul but everything. Not just our churches and Christian gatherings in buildings, but everything.

When you pray, pray like this, 'your kingdom come, your will be done, on earth as it is in heaven' [Matthew 6:10]. Heaven is the domain where God gets His own way. Pray that God would get His own way on earth. This place here, this land right here, the mud, the earth that we stand upon right now. May Your Kingship come here, God. May this place that we are standing on, living on, walking about on … May Your kingdom come! May Your will be done here. May *shalom* be restored to *this* place. When you pray, pray about God getting His way in the place where you are living right now!

'Seek the *shalom* of the place that I have carried you into.'

He didn't say get praying for God that [you get] to heaven when you die, He said pray that He would bring heaven to earth right now, He would bring *shalom* here, pray it for your land. Pray it for your city, your workplaces, your streets, your council, your hospitals and your schools. God, have Your way … here, in my land.

So, in Babylon, what do you do when you find that you are living in a land that does not know God? A city where the dome of God's Kingship has not come, a place where the brokenness of *shalom* is really obvious? What do you do there? The call of this passage is that you are to live there, do regular everyday life in that place, wash the dishes, go to work, buy stuff from the shops, do the school run, join the local football team and while you are living there, 'Seek the *shalom* of that land.' Spend your lives working towards the kingdom transformation of that land, right there.

My land is Teesside, Middlesborough and Stockton; this is the land that we are in and are commanded to seek its *shalom*. This is the earth that [we] stand upon as we pray 'on earth as it is in heaven' [Matthew 6:10]. That's what the Church is, the people of God who are of this *shalom*, those whom God has placed in the cities. The Church, you see, isn't about the Church. For too long the Church has been about the Church. How do we make the Church better, how do we make the Church more like this or like that, how do we spend more money on the Church, how do we gather more people in the Church, how do we grow the Church?

The Church isn't about the Church; it never has been and it never should be. The Church is all about God becoming King again, on this earth, on this land here, where we are, where we are placed, where we are called to, God becoming King in Stockton again. God becoming King in Teesside again, *shalom* being restored in this land right here.

We will not see [the] kingdom come while we are looking inwards at our own individual churches, hoping that this year a few more people with come to our Sunday services if our band practises more and our preacher steps up his game. I believe that kingdom will come to a real extent when we lift our eyes and see what Jesus sees when He looks over Teesside. He sees His Church. One Church. His people, scattered out across this land, like salt rubbed into every nook and cranny ... Ready to bring flavour to it. *Shalom*-seekers working in education in our city. *Shalom* seekers rubbed into the healthcare systems in our city. *Shalom*-seekers in shopping centres, *shalom*-seekers down streets and in care homes and in small businesses.

He sees one Church with different gatherings, different styles, beautiful variety, but one Church, one people, one body, on a kingdom *shalom* mission. We are united because we have the same King and we have been given the same mission from that King.

Do you know what I think needs to happen? I think that we need to stop seeing ourselves in these small silos with walls and barriers of differences between us. I think that we need to start thinking of ourselves as one Church. This means that if you are a teacher working for the *shalom* of the education systems of this land, then you need to start gathering with others who are also seeking the *shalom* of the education systems of this land. If you are a nurse and you have given your life to seeing kingdom come over the healthcare in this land, and there are others who have given their lives to that very same thing, then it's a no-brainer that you would want to and need to be meeting and praying and talking and encouraging each other. Business leaders grabbing a hold of other business leaders and saying, 'You are one of Jesus' people, seeking His kingdom in business: where do you do that, then? In Stockton? That's my land.' Same King, same mission, same land.

Forget your denominations and whether you like incense or guitars on a Sunday morning. This is a no-brainer: the people of God starting to work together on His mission because they are in the same land.

Because here we are in the same land, we are on the same mission. To whom did Paul write when he wrote letters to the growing movement of house churches? He wrote to the Church in Rome, the Church in Ephesus, the Church in Corinth. Not one house church. But the people of God on mission in that land.

Just before Christmas, a group of twenty-five church leaders from Middlesbrough met for the morning. Church leaders of gatherings of all sorts of different styles and traditions; if we had been talking about communion, or worship music or baptism, we would have had a lot of different answers given. But do you know what we talked about? We asked the question, 'What would it look like if Jesus was King in our city?' If Jesus got His way with our land, what would it look like?

And do you know what? All of us completely agreed with each other's answers. We are one because we have the same King and He has given us the same mission and we are in the same land. There is a great awakening happening all over the world right now. The walls that used to be so high between denominations and so focused on differences are now crumbling and people are starting to see their Christian brothers and sisters for who they really are. They are partners in the same mission, with the same King, and they are placed in the same land as we are.

We are one. One people, one King, one mission, in the same land.

As you go forward as the Church in this land, let me challenge you to joined-up thinking. Who else is on this mission around us, whom else can we partner with, whom else can we be friends with and support and encourage and work with? Because we are in the same land on the same mission. The Church in Teesside.

Every Tuesday morning, the church leaders in Middlesbrough pray together. We have been doing this for five years now, and let me tell you my entire ministry has changed! On Tuesday morning it's like the beginning of my week and it's like meeting my staff team. The guys and ladies that are on the same mission as me, in the same town as me, praying, sharing, encouraging, planning, scheming together, Catholics, Free Church, Methodists, Baptists, Anglicans, Pentecostals. They are my team.

Chapter 7
The New Church for the
New City

What does a city-transformational church and leader look like?

The transforming God is bringing about His kingdom in all sectors and aspects of life. This fundamental ongoing change is also coming to the Church.

We are blessed by a fundamental reformation that has happened to the Church over the last few decades. The ecumenical movement challenged and changed how we related to each other's denominations. The charismatic movement was a breath of fresh air across the stuffy institutional, frozen denominations. The social action movement from the liberal tradition has now taken hold in the evangelical Pentecostal family and mission is now on the agenda again.

All these movements to greater or lesser degrees have shaken the core practices and changed structures of how local churches operate and do life together. I believe with this gathering momentum of unity for the transformation of the city arising all over the world we will begin to see another reshaping of the Church.

What would happen if we intentionally grew local churches to reach and affect a city, working alongside others in the wider body of Christ? How would our mindset, practices, theology change?

As a pastor of a local church, I entered ministry with a basic paradigm.

- Grow the church: my first aim was to grow the local congregation numerically as quickly as possible. If it grew, I would be a success at this new job. This growth would ideally come from new converts finding faith but I was more than happy accepting new members from Christians moving into the area, or even from other churches; in fact, secretly I felt that if the grass was greener on my side of the fence, that again would define my success levels.

- Pastor the people: my second priority was to pastor and teach this group of people to help them navigate the trials of life and to keep their faith as vital as possible.

- Support the network: my main point of reference outside the local church was my denominational family, in my case, the Baptists. They took any time I had left for wider ministry and I saw it was my role to support that family.

- Evangelise: in term of mission in the late 1980s and early 1990s, I was very focused on evangelism, with a well thought-through process of enabling people along the Engel Scale of interest in Jesus to conversion and discipleship. Seekers' services became a very effective stepping stone along the way towards conversion and under God's grace we saw many come to faith. I appreciated the wider aspect of mission that members developed, such as feeding the homeless and welcoming children and families going through messy divorces, but the priority was always evangelism.

- Get them involved: although I never really said it out loud, I really viewed the people who were part of the church as God's gifts to the church. I was focused on them developing their gifts and callings, but my paradigm was that this gifting was mainly to stay inside the church. I think I understood if a few people had special callings outside the church, like running a major corporation or being a local councillor or even being a senior emergency doctor. I blessed them in their activity but deep down felt they were not really part of my remit because they couldn't get to church and serve as much as others.

- Live in your own world: while I placed a great deal of emphasis on our members building friendships with their non-Christian friends and praying for opportunities to share faith and invite them to numerous guest events, I certainly had no contact with any other third-sector agency, council department or other statutory department. I had no need to be connected with them. We were growing our church, we were doing some good deeds, but in complete isolation from any other body or organisation.

- Church unity: in regard to working with other churches, my experience of this was to get along with them in peace, turn up at an event every now and then, and mind my own business.

I'm not proud of this paradigm but I don't beat myself up about it. I think I was partly a product of the evangelical charismatic culture of the time; my theology was limited and my vision was insular. The ministry was not without its fruit, significant number of people came to faith, many people grew in their walk with Christ, and people experienced personal transformation.

However, as missional as the church was, my own journey and the journey of many in this book has been a long one over many years as God has opened us up to a much wider perspective and challenged fundamentally how we think about what we do.

What have been the main paradigm change factors?

1. The context of living in an increasingly secular, postmodern and non-Christian state has led to some fundamental development in missional practice and theology. How do you influence people who have very little understanding of the Christian Faith and the Church, which for most is so culturally relegated it is irrelevant. This context has led to a fresh understanding of contextual mission, asking hard questions of what we are doing, what we are saying and how we live.

2. Our understanding of the Bible has deepened, particularly in regard to eschatology and mission. The parameters of understanding Christ's victory have widened to include not just the establishment of the local church and its growth through evangelism, but also the gathering in of all creation under Christ, the establishment of the kingdom through justice, truth, freedom and love; the renewal of the heaven and earth. This is a big picture gospel that includes every aspect and facet of the complex modern city.

3. The very important work of the LICC and other whole-life discipleship-focused agencies has begun to seriously challenge the paradigm that church members are mainly the engine of the church. They have argued strongly for a better perspective of seeing the people of God as the dispersed Church on the frontline in the workplaces and neighbourhoods of society, actively seeking to bring in the kingdom to effect social, spiritual and cultural change.

4. The growing understanding of place and the importance of the bigger vision to see the transformation of cities and towns is changing our success criteria and context. How can a church leader effect kingdom change in business or the health service? However, their church members are well positioned to effect that change if resourced, motivated, envisioned and enabled.

I believe a significant movement is now occurring where God is moving the local church towards a wider and more expansive paradigm. It is not that we now have to leave behind all the key foundations of the previous paradigm, but we do have to undergo a major refurbishment and extension of our practice and vision.

So, what are the main hallmarks of transformational Church, and what are the sort of leaders we must grow to lead these churches?

The hallmarks of a city-wide transforming church

1. Creating loving communities in lonely places

> We serve the world by showing it something it is not, namely a place where God is forming a family out of strangers.
> *Stanley Hauerwas*[19]

To pray and work for the transformation of our places we must first become the transformation that we are talking about. If we want to see our places become safer and more peaceful, free from abuse and crime, with healthy families and strong social cohesion, with less inequality and division, we must, as Jesus says, become God's city set on the hill (Matthew 5:14), an example and vision of how we should live together. This is why Paul, after his epic vision of the authority of Christ and the role of the Church in the first chapters of Ephesians, at the end of the book concentrates on how the Church must live together. With

[19] Stanley Hauerwas and William H Willimon, *Resident Aliens* (Nashville, TN: Abingdon Press, 1989), pp82-83.

its focus on relationships, the integrated body of Christ, living as children of the light, 'holy and blameless' (Ephesians 5:27), with a commitment to mutual submission and love.

As a leader and creator of many programmes in church life over the years, I've become acutely aware that sometimes it is easier to create and run a programme than it is to build a loving community. I am sometimes worried that we are replacing the basic building blocks of creating loving life-giving communities with a set of strategic programmes. I thank God for all the courses, initiatives and social action projects being developed that have helped give focus and support to the work of the local church. However, I believe they are additional to the fundamental nature and vision of the church which is to worship God, build the body and make disciples. As a pastor I know that it is sometimes easier to run a project or to lead a new initiative than it is to do the hard slog of building strong relationships within the body, developing a life-giving relational culture and dealing with the difficult issues that challenge that culture.

One of the most serious challenges of Western urbanisation and increased mobility is the erosion of community life, and alongside this erosion is the fracturing of family relationships which is resulting in higher and higher levels of loneliness and isolation. People have less and less of a sense of belonging, being part of a place and a context that centre them, creating support structures that serve them through difficult times. My own city of

Manchester recently reported[20] that 35 per cent of its young residents were lonely and 27 per cent of all residents. This has serious consequences for the care of the elderly, the pressure placed on the health service and the rates of self-harm and suicide.

This is increasingly a world in need of friendship and community, and the Church is well placed to meet that growing need. Where else can you find a group of strangers who are actively building community together, old and young, able and disabled, black and white, socialist and conservative? One of our greatest and perhaps most mysterious strengths is the simple existence of loving communities in virtually every neighbourhood of the land. These ordinary and yet at the same time extraordinary communities shine as a light to the kingdom and a place of welcome and healing for all. They are, of course, not perfect; they have their struggles and challenges, sometimes they fail in building community and hurt each other, sometimes they could be so much more than they are. However, even in their imperfection they still yearn for and work towards growing better more loving communities.

This golden thread of community life must be constantly nurtured and prioritised in our church life; it is the place where we will show much of the love of God to the world. Jesus said, 'By this everyone will know that you are my disciples, if you love one another' (John 13:35). Our projects and programmes will have little to no effect if they

---

[20] http://www.manchestereveningnews.co.uk/news/greater-manchester-news/greater-manchester-men-survey-results-12756713 (accessed 6th July 2017).

are not infused with the love of God expressed between His people and overflowing to the world. Our cities need loving – we are not here to conquer them, to take them for Christ; we are here to wrap the loving arms of God around them. We will only do that if we ourselves know that love, practise that love between us and then allow it to overflow from us to others. Our cities need community: they need to have people and places they feel safe in and they belong to.

One of the most effective ways to build vibrant communities is to begin to plant new churches. This calls for a strategic and coordinated approach to church planting, a joined-up conversation between all the churches across a region, asking the question, 'Where is the need and who is best placed to respond?' Some denominations are closing churches at a significant rate and some communities now no longer have a robust witness to Christ. It is time that this joined-up conversation does not just happen within the denominations, but between the denominations. If a church has to close, the very first requirement should be to talk with the wider body of Christ to see if someone else could begin a vibrant community living out a message of love in lonely places.

2. Making whole-life disciples to effect kingdom change

If we are to see significant social and cultural change in our towns and cities, we need to refocus our efforts on reaching people spiritually with the gospel, seeing them begin their journey into faith and then growing them into mature disciples who follow Christ into the world to be city-changers.

In my home land of Nigeria we have many millions of people who have found faith in Christ. Nigeria is over 50 per cent a Christian nation with over 30 per cent evangelical believers and yet it is a country riddled with corruption, crime and poverty. It is not enough to see converts, we need to see transformed disciples who are transforming society.

African leader from Liverpool

My daughter Naomi and son-in-law Scott, when looking for a church to belong to, attended some in the new area they had moved to. When asked what they did, they replied that she was a primary school teacher and he was a builder. When people in one of the churches found out, they became very welcoming and interested, obviously seeing their arrival as an answer to prayer for the much-needed support in the Sunday school and the many practical building jobs that needed to be done. However, Naomi teaches in one of the most deprived and challenging areas in the country, and Scott is a small business owner.

Surely the vision we have for our church members must be larger than the needs of the local congregation. I want my daughter and son-in-law to find a church that sees them as precious God-made people who have significant potential to affect people's lives. I want Naomi to be the very best teacher she can be, serving some of the most disadvantaged and damaged kids in the country. I want Scott to be a very good businessman, providing employment, setting high standards of workmanship and making people's homes more beautiful. They will, of course, serve in their church, but it's not the main place they will fulfil their callings, it is not the main area of impact they will have in life.

A city-transforming church sees its primary role as being to bless the place God has called them to, to be part of the wider body of Christ, to see more and more of God's kingdom come in their town or city. As has been stated before, the vision is to see transformation come into all areas, sectors and spheres of life. A local school and its educational achievements are as much the focus of attention as a church's Sunday school. Thriving businesses create employment, prosperity and stability in an area, and a great health service gives hope to many who are suffering from illness.

Jesus called us to be the yeast in the dough (Matthew 13:33), to effect significant change slowly over time, to be people of integrity, stability, vision and love. As local church leaders, we need to see our role as producing the quality of disciple who will be that yeast in society. We need to rejoice when our people become exemplary neighbours, faithful workers in the local hospital and outstanding businesspeople.

3. A big city vision in a world of small dreams

One of the essential hallmarks of a transformational church is to lift up your vision beyond your own patch, parish and local area to the wider picture of the town or city. This is the vision of the God of Jonah and Nehemiah, it's the heart of Christ as He cries out for Jerusalem, it's the focus of Paul as he travels to all the main cities of the Roman Empire.

One of the main reasons we've not done this before is because of our limited understanding of the body of Christ. If we see ourselves as leaders of local churches linked to our national denominational network with a limited number of other networked churches close to us, we will always be blind to the city vision. We will always see this vision as beyond us, impossible and unattainable. However, if we see ourselves as part of the whole body of Christ, called to enable and release our people into society, we can begin to raise our vision beyond our patch to the wider town or city.

No one church will effect significant kingdom change across a town or city, but together in unity, and releasing and networking our people in the spheres of life, we can begin to gain some imagination for transformation.

4. Knowing and feeling for your place

God asks Jonah, 'should I not have concern for the great city of Nineveh, in which there are more than a hundred and twenty thousand people?' (Jonah 4:11); 'As [Jesus] approached Jerusalem and saw the city, he wept over it' (Luke 19:41); '"The wall of Jerusalem is broken down, and its gates have been burned with fire." When I heard these things, I sat down and wept' (Nehemiah 1:3-4).

If we are to take seriously the calling of God to go into His world with the good news, we must gain a much deeper knowledge of the places where God has sent us. Every town or city has a distinct history and culture with assets, strengths and challenges. Having had the privilege of travelling across the country talking with city leaders, I am surprised at the uniqueness of every place. Each has a strong narrative of where it came from, its story of development and sometimes decline, its personality and culture, its setting and types of people.

A hallmark of transformational churches is to know our places. This is key tenet in missiology, to know the people and context you are operating in. How well do we know our places?

Here is a list of some of the key questions we should know about:

a.   Population demographics (age, ethnic mix, religious affiliation, etc);

b.   Social and economic mix;

c.   Health and well-being, strengths and challenges;

d.   Education attainment;

e.   Crime and safety issues;

f.   Economic, employment and skills levels;

g.   Housing context;

h.   The strength or weakness of the cultural sector;

i.   The environmental challenges;

j.   The fifteen- to twenty-year vision for the town or city;

k.   The list of the main assets of the area;

l.   The history and how the place thinks about life and itself;

m.   The spiritual story of the area;

n. The state of the public sector, its work and its main challenges;

o. The state of the third sector, its work and its main challenges.

Much of this information will be held by the relevant public bodies and is easily available, and most towns and cities have local history groups who will give huge amounts of information. A lot of the softer knowledge, such as how a place views itself, can be collated from your own members and general pastoral ministry. The process of gaining this information will lead you to have conversations with civic leaders and often lead to forming some important friendships going forwards.

Once gained, this information is crucial in setting a mission strategy. It will better inform you as to the needs of the area and the opportunities for the churches to serve within. If undertaken with all the churches, we will have less duplication and more strategic focus. This exercise is also an opportunity to build relationships with wider civic life, and move from doing 'mission to' people and 'for' people to doing 'mission with' the people of the area.

In addition to knowing your places better, there is also the challenge of feeling for the places God has placed us within. Nehemiah's first reaction to the knowledge of the state of the walls in his home city was not to form a strategy but to weep and mourn and fast. Jesus, when seeing the state of Jerusalem, was deeply moved. He didn't just see the demographics, He saw people as sheep without a shepherd who were harassed and helpless. Knowing a city is to feel the heart God has for the city, to feel the anguish and challenges and then be moved towards action. It is Dietrich Bonhoeffer who said, 'action springs not from thought but from a readiness for responsibility'.[21] Responsibility is felt, it is something that grabs you in the guts, as it did Jesus.

One of the most beneficial things you can do is to walk around your area, to get out and simply walk in an attitude of prayer over a period of time, to listen spiritually to the place you have been called to serve. To ask God to give you His heart for it. To feel the pain and issues facing the people you are called to serve.

5.   Part of the place, no longer isolated

For too long in our church community, we were isolated from the rest of the structures and organisations in the borough. We lived a dualistic approach to ministry that saw what we did as the most spiritual and therefore most important, and what the police or health bodies or council departments did as important but not really our business. So we had little to no contact with any civic authority or other charity in the borough. We did our own thing without any reference to anybody, and ploughed our own furrow.

If we are, however, to see our places transformed, we must begin to operate with those who share the same vision and purpose. Some talk about working alongside people of goodwill, or people of peace – those who may not

---

[21] Dietrich Bonhoeffer, *Letters and Papers from Prison* (New York: Touchstone, 1997) (first published 1951).

share your faith but do share a heart for the town or city and want to see it flourish and develop.

Our own journey as local church started, extraordinarily, in Uganda when involved in a mission trip to Jinja. For some reason we got invited into the town hall to meet the mayor and all his councillors who then proceeded to ask to be twinned with our borough of Trafford in Greater Manchester. I wasn't sure how to respond but simply said that when I met our mayor I would ask him. This was relatively easy to say, since I had never in ten years met the mayor of Trafford. However, six months later I did meet the mayor, and felt duty-bound to pass on the request. He was very enthusiastic and was soon leading a delegation to Uganda alongside our regular church team. The fruit of this one request over the next twenty years was staggering, resulting in significant partnership with all the civic authorities, the provision of a building from which to operate a major community centre, and opportunity to help lead the borough at a senior level. Alongside this, the opportunity has arisen many times to share faith and see people come closer to Christ. We have become part of the structure and organisation of the city, with strong growing relationships with city leaders and civic institutions.

6. In the wider body of Christ

A church that has a broader, more ambitious vision to see significant change across a town or city will soon realise that this cannot be achieved by any one church or organisation. It is ridiculous to think that effective long-term change can be done in isolation from others within the body of Christ even without recognising the biblical call to unity.

The body of Christ image used by Paul in 1 Corinthians 12:12-31 is often only applied to a local church setting or across a denomination. However, this was an image written to a major city in the first century, with many expressions of Church across it. The image of the body is very relevant even in today's context. It warns strongly against independence, with feet and eyes declaring self-sufficiency from the rest of the body. It warns against treating lesser, more modest parts of the body with anything but respect and honour. It alerts the body to feel empathy when one part suffers, and not to be indifferent.

Like the human body, the body of Christ is diverse and multifaceted, with each part playing its role, with its own importance and place. We all need each other, we need the life and vitality of the Pentecostals and charismatics, we need the social justice dimension of the Methodists, the depth of the Catholics and the position of the Church of England within civic life. We need different churches that can attract young people, families and elderly people. We need places for extroverts and introverts, varying ethnicities and different social classes. We need churches that can focus on the very poor, others that can focus on releasing their people in strategic places to make policy changes towards the poor. We need large churches to push ahead in major new missional projects and we need smaller, more local churches to enculturate the gospel within their communities. We need Christian organisations to target particular needs within the city and to pull in major resources nationally to make a difference. We need intercessory groups and houses of prayer to commit themselves to praying for the whole town and its needs. We need Christians in all sectors of life to be a faithful presence where God has called them. We need everybody to play their part in God's mission to bring transformation.

The movements we have spoken about in this book who deeply believe in this biblical picture of unity are beginning to see some transformation happen.

7. Growing a creative and adventurous church culture following the leading of the Holy Spirit

As the Church increasingly engages in the needs, pain and aspirations of the city, it must increasingly contextualise its mission for its place. As good as national initiatives, strategies and off-the-shelf ministries are, they must always take second place to a local creative and contextual mission. A multicultural city such as Bradford will need a very different approach from a town in the Cotswolds; Haringey is a world away from Poole in Dorset. One size does not fit all, and one approach is not the answer to every need.

One of my concerns in regard to mission is the lack of creativity and Holy Spirit-led adventurous mission. We seem too eager at times to repeat what others have done, or simply keep doing what we do because it seems to have worked in the past. We need a new missional imagination that is created out of the context and culture of the locality and responds to the needs of the people who live there.

Linked to this, we need to grow a culture of risk and adventure to try new things, to invest in the ideas of our members, and especially the young people. Creativity can only grow in the atmosphere of trial and error, piloted programmes and relational trust. Failure must become second nature to us, we must be prepared to fall on our faces in defeat, to pick ourselves up and learn from the situation. It was Dyson who took five years and 5,127 failed prototypes before his breakthrough in the vacuum cleaner.

Creative mission grows out of understanding and respect for context and the need for creating a culture of risk and adventure, but it also arises from a commitment to follow the still small voice of the Spirit. True kingdom transformation will arise once we begin to follow the missionary God into His world; it is God who speaks His word of life across the places of desolation and ruin. It is God who creates the new day, the new beginning. His is the ever-creative force behind the universe, still making and generating.

8. Intentional focus of serving the most vulnerable in the city

Once a church begins to take seriously the needs and aspirations of its area, it will become very aware that there is so much opportunity to serve. In the UK, the options are ever-increasing. What should the Church be doing? Some are running libraries, others are commissioned to serve older people or run a youth service. The choices are increasingly multifaceted, so what should we be doing or not doing? The answer is that obviously each church has to make its own decisions under the guidance of the Holy Spirit; however, Scripture does give us general overall guidance, and that is to choose to serve the most vulnerable, those most at risk and in need.

9. Releasing substantial resources to the city vision

A church that is serious about the transformation of its town or city must outwork that responsibility in financial giving, as well as the release of people. Local churches have a good track record in releasing money towards their own local mission and discipleship of their people; they also take responsibility regarding their national denominations, and most churches operate a world missions' budget, giving generously to other nations. However, if we are beginning to see the context of the city or the town we have been placed in as an essential and important part of the mission we are called to, then money and time needs to be given to enable this to be fulfilled.

Leading a city-based transformational church

It takes a special leader to create a local church designed to reach a city. A significant paradigm change is needed in perspective and success criteria. Here are some of the hallmarks of this new type of leader.

1. Developing a kingdom mentality

Developing a kingdom and not an empire mentality is the first step in growing a city-transforming mindset. I use the word 'empire' to describe a strong-growing, well-shaped entity with borders, purpose and cohesion. It exists for its own sake to expand and become ever more powerful and influential. At its worst, in church terms this is typified by an attitude and approach that can come over as self-sufficient, self-interested and self-absorbed. An empire-based local church would have little to do with other churches, interact minimally with other partners, and essentially do its own thing. It's holding its own party and others can come and join in, but it's usually on its own terms and in its own home.

Unfortunately, I've seen this attitude in local churches, denominations, mission agencies and Christian charities. I know this attitude, because at times I've sadly lived it myself. Leading a larger church can have its temptations that can affect your spirit. You can start to believe in your own publicity and success, creating an impression that you are God's gift to the Christian world. This can lead to other members of the Christian family feeling pushed away, patronised and excluded. I think it needs to be stated strongly that such an empire-based attitude is essentially sinful; it lacks humility, love and the biblical command of considering others better than yourself. It goes against the picture that Paul paints of the body with its different parts all working together, all valued and vital to the overall creation.

Developing a kingdom attitude, I think, expresses a very different paradigm. It's not about my or our empire, it's all about His kingdom, His reign over all creation. We are caught up in God's purposes to bring about His rulership over all the earth. We are to seek this kingdom, to give our lives for it wherever we see it, wherever it needs to be established.

In this kingdom expansion I am invited to play my small part, but only in terms of serving a higher authority and being part of His body.

The powerful Methodist covenant prayer clearly states this humble attitude:

I am no longer my own but yours.
Put me to what you will,
rank me with whom you will;
put me to doing, put me to suffering;
let me be employed for you, or laid aside for you,
exalted for you, or brought low for you.
Let me be full, let me be empty,
let me have all things, let me have nothing:
I freely and wholeheartedly yield all things
to your pleasure and disposal.[22]

If the kingdom of God is to come across more fully in the places we live in, it has to be lived and seen in His Church. The values and practices of the kingdom are about self-denial, service of others, gentleness, loving the vulnerable, taking the lesser role and humbling ourselves under His hand.

Kingdom leaders that are growing kingdom churches are always looking to serve other churches and leaders; they are humble in their attitude, not seeking to be the most well known, admired and powerful. They obviously take responsibility for their part of the vineyard, they must express their gifts and become all they were created to become, but not at the expense of others. Kingdom leaders are always looking to form partnerships, work alongside and learn from others. They have a willingness to submit

[22] http://www.methodist.org.uk/who-we-are/what-is-distinctive-about-methodism/a-covenant-with-god (accessed 21st June 2017).

their own plans, sometimes at their own expense, in order to see a greater outcome for the kingdom.

2. Developing a love and dependence on the whole body of Christ

One of the drivers for an empire mentality is a valuing of an independent approach to ministry. Personally, I found this in the past linked to my own personal needs for affirmation. If the church grew, I felt better about myself; if that growth was linked more and more to me individually as the leader, then so much the better. However, it is a huge challenge to all this ego-based ministry to see myself as one pastor in a large city among many others. It is a challenge to my independence to be called into the body of Christ to become interdependent, to need the support and help of others. Once this uncomfortable ego barrier can be broken through, life becomes a lot easier. What a joy to be part of city-wide team, each with our own strengths and gifting, able to learn from each other, support one another. What a delight to go into other churches and say to myself, 'This isn't necessarily my cup of tea, but what can I see of Jesus here? What can I learn and take back to my context?' Having spent some time with my African brothers and sisters, I may not feel at home in their specific cultural context, but I've learned so much about fasting, giving and prayer. From constantly comparing myself to others in ministry, what a relief to be able to simply look out for the best in each other, affirming and building each other up to become friends and not just colleagues, to have a place to go to, to have safe people to share with.

3. Taking responsibility for the city or town

One of the key hallmarks of a leader of a city-transformational church is that they begin, with others, to take spiritual responsibility for their place. The people, the infrastructure and its future are in their prayers: they are part of what they think about and work for. This is essentially a wider parish mentality where we lift our eyes towards a wider horizon. This challenges an all too common mentality that church pastoral ministry is about caring for the flock, my church members, building the institution and doing some good things for the community. However, if what I am responsible for, with others, is the whole town, then this changes everything. Am I now a pastor to the whole city? Am I now an integral part of the services delivered to the community, with the council and others? Am I to have a concern, a deeply moving compassion towards the area, such as God had to Nineveh (Jonah 4:11)? Should I now ring-fence time and resources to this wider responsibility? Will this change my diary and commitments?

The answer is yes to all the above. This isn't easy, it won't be without stresses and challenges, but it is a hallmark of a city pastor.

4. Focus on the long-term goal of a transformed city

I was never really sure what success looked like as a pastor, but, over twenty-two years of ministry within one church, I become aware that most people in and outside the church asked about how many people you had attending, how much money you raised and gave away, and what sort of building you had. Those with a big budget and large attendance and state-of-the-art buildings were obviously more successful. It's not that those issues aren't relevant; it is important that we grow churches, particularly through conversion growth; it is vital that we raise and release finance for the kingdom, and it is helpful to have buildings that are fit for purpose.

However, Jesus seems to prioritise the making of disciples and the mission of bringing His kingdom to the places we live in. Those criteria of success (if success is the right word) are much more about quality than quantity. They are about depth and impact, rather than surface issues. The making of disciples is a lifelong venture; the encouragement to them to be the best wife, mother and artist they can be will take time and effort. To begin to see them affecting their neighbourhoods and workplaces is a long-term, quality, focused ministry. This is about long-lasting, great-tasting fruit, and it will only come when we value that more deeply than the other less important, more superficial success criteria. Growing a church focused on reaching a city is about growing the people who will be able to do that; it's about developing long-term relationships in the wider society; it's about being part of a wider group of leaders. And together over time you will see the effect and it will be more strategic and more effective than the former paradigm.

5. Transformation is personal
The dream of city-wide transformation through a transformed Church will only come about through transformed leaders. Transformation is all about change and growth; it's about repentance, turning around,

changing direction; it's about foreignness and spiritual growth; it's about love and commitment; it's about being in love with Jesus and in an ongoing, ever-growing relationship with Him. If we want to see people come to Christ and be transformed, if we want to see business change and become more honest and responsible, if we want to see education develop and be transformed, and much more besides, this change we seek in others must first be real in our own lives.

It's so easy to do the things of ministry, to preach about growth and faith, to encourage others to put aside pride and walk away from sin and not actively be in that place ourselves. The challenge of leading a transformational church is to be ourselves the river of God's transformational work. Conversion is not a once-and-for-all occurrence; we are constantly being saved from ourselves; our minds, it says in Romans 12:2, should be constantly transformed. We are the pilgrims on the journey to Christ; we are the players on the pitch, not the supporters in the stands. Any commitment to city-wide transformation is a commitment to a deeper, more intentional relationship with the Transformer of all things.

A city leader leading a city-focused church is paying attention to their own soul, listening and responding to the work of Christ in them personally. Many have found meeting in close prayer/growth groups to be very helpful in this personal development, such as they have set up in Chester and Watford. Others find time for regular retreats, or spiritual direction. Whatever support works best for you, it's vital that, as you call a church to this wider vision, and call a city closer to God, you yourself must live the message.

Beatitudes for transformational church leaders, by Nic Harding (Unity leader in Liverpool)

1. Blessed are the unity-minded for they will be blessed with many friends on the journey.

2. Blessed are those who equip their members as they will have an exciting church.

3. Blessed are those who weep over their city as they will see God move.

4. Blessed are those who invest in raising leaders as they will grow and multiply their church.

5. Blessed are those who lead by example as they will have the reward of a peaceful heart.

6. Blessed are those who focus outwardly as they will grow inwardly.

7. Blessed are those who demonstrate the gospel as they will have the right to speak about it.

8. Blessed are those who see the kingdom, not just the Church, as they will be the culture-changers.

Chapter 8
The New Partnership

How churches should engage with civic society

A CEO of a local council recently described the current round of austerity cuts hitting local government as the greatest crisis affecting local communities since the war. With many councils now having reduced their spending by up to 33 per cent, they are now facing another 50 per cent cut over the next five years. These level of reductions are also being felt in the police force, the third sector and other social institutions, with education and health probably to follow close behind. The basic civic agreement with citizens is under threat, with many local authorities wondering how it will be able to meet even their statutory responsibilities to the young and the elderly.

The Church has an opportunity to increase its service to local areas in this growing vacuum in social support, since unlike other organisations, the Church relies less on grant funding and more on the generosity of its members. The Church is essential to the warp and weft of social capital in every area with its pastoral care, toddlers' groups, elderly support, youth provision, food banks and many more services.

For many years, the door to more significant partnership with secular bodies was often closed. Suspicion, ignorance and sometimes even hostility was the experience of churches as they approached their civic authorities. However, now the door in most places is well and truly open. If civic authorities are to survive, they must partner and outsource as much as possible and the Church is one group that is being courted as a key partner for the future. We are increasingly being seen as an effective way to reach local communities that others find hard to reach, with a long-term track record in neighbourhoods, with concrete resources in buildings and staff, and a significant voluntary force at our disposal.

Over the last five years, there is much evidence of churches taking this opportunity: costly civic assets are being transferred, youth services are being outsourced, work among the most needy families is being commissioned, and much more.

The landscape has changed and will be changing for at least the next five years; there hasn't been an opportunity like this in decades for churches to engage in civic life.

With opportunity, of course, comes risk, and Luke Bretherton in his book *Christianity & Contemporary Politics*[23] is right to warn us about avoiding the dangers of being co-opted to serve others' agendas we may not be comfortable serving, or being forced into competition for funding

[23] Luke Bretherton, *Christianity & Contemporary Politics: The Conditions and Possibilities of Faithful Witness* (Hoboken, NJ: Wiley-Blackwell, 2010).

against other churches, or being coerced into losing our faith dimension in order to gain more funding. We may also become part of the new establishment and distance ourselves from our independent prophetic calling. Pride and power will be the new dangers for this next period, following several decades of marginalisation and impotence.

This chapter originates from a meeting with some key experienced practitioners who are walking this tightrope by serving in the civic sphere and trying to avoid the dangers above. More than seventy key leaders met together in March 2013 at the Gather 'Working Together' consultation, regarding how Church can connect with civic authorities. The room was full of church leaders and Christians who have extensive experience in working with councils, the health sector, housing associations, the police, colleges, leisure trusts and other third-sector organisations.

Most of them operate alongside or within Gather-type unity movements that are documented in this book. They are increasingly asking the question: 'What could happen over the next thirty years if the Church got its act together, working in collaborative strategic unity for the sake of the place we have been called to; could we see lasting transformation of our towns and cities?'

These golden nuggets of advice for civic engagement emerge from that missional perspective; these are not helpful hints for short-term projects but values that need to grow over a long time, cultures that need to be created over twenty to thirty years, relationships that need to become long-lasting friendships.

Understand this is a new day

There was a time when churches may have been treated with some suspicion and ignorance by civic authorities, and there was a general unwillingness to engage. That attitude has fundamentally changed in most places over the last few years. Participants at the consultation spoke encouragingly about the new opportunities being afforded them, and a new respect for the work of the churches. Churches are seen as a significant service providers, with staff, buildings and large numbers of volunteers. The financial crisis has now given even more impetus for authorities to partner with churches. With budgets being cut, they are having to find new ways of delivering services and the door is wide open for dialogue, partnership and effective engagement. There hasn't been an opportunity like this for decades, and it's time for the Church to walk into this arena with humble confidence and seek to serve the city to which it has been called.

Do it in unity

The consultation involved some of the key unity movements around the country who are effectively engaging with the civic authorities, and they all underlined the importance of approaching the statutory authorities as a group of united churches, and not just as individual churches. The authorities want one phone number to ring, one group to deal with, not several individual churches all competing for time and resources. It is not only strategic to do things in as joined-up a way as possible, but it is, of course, witness to the gospel that when we are in unity we better express the love God has for this world.

Go to the top and work down

Take the initiative and ask to meet with the chief executive and leader of the council, or the chief superintendent of the police, or the CEO of the housing trust. If you go as a small team on behalf of other churches, they are often more than willing to have a conversation with you. Try to begin the engagement at this level, then work down to the more local and junior level. If you get the buy-in with those in most authority, it will make your local work much easier. It's important, of course, to work with local civic leaders and officers on the ground, but often they need encouragement from the top before they can commit time and resources to local needs.

Ask them what they need

Don't focus so much on your needs as churches, but go to the authorities and engage them in a conversation specifically asking them about their key priorities. Ask them to give you three things they are concerned about and you could possibly help them with. You may not be able to meet all those needs but you should be able to meet some of them. We are here to be a blessing to the place God has called us to, and not a drain on it. The authorities often feel pressurised by local groups and charities to serve their own priorities; it will be a welcome conversation for them to be asked about *their* challenges and how the Church can partner in serving society.

Be professional

Be professional in your approach, do your research into whom you are meeting and what you want to talk to them about. Make yourself aware of other third-sector organisations operating in your community, what other statutory authorities are involved, and the agreed action plans already in place. You need to avoid being seen to be amateur in your approach, or needlessly duplicating services others are providing.

Deal with the elephant in the room

If they do have hesitations about working with you, it may be because they have had experience with some church groups who sought to use public money to proselytise, or who were not inclusive in the service they offered. It's often best at the start of the engagement to name the elephant in the room and deal with these misconceptions.

It's important to state that you are here to serve everyone and not just one group and that, although sharing your faith is important to you, you will not use publicly funded initiatives to do that. If the people you serve wish to connect with your other church activities, then they are very welcome, but assure them no one will be forced or coerced into church. If there is a very negative history, you may need to go into much more detail and develop a code of practice.

Building relationships is vital

A long-lasting fruitful engagement will only be achieved through building strong relationships with the key civic leaders in your area. This is simply about making friends beyond the meetings, taking an interest in their lives and serving them when needed. It's about a calling to be pastors of the area, not only of the Church, to care and pray for people with significant leadership responsibility.

This friendship will also be a two-way relationship and you will learn so much about providing services, leadership skills and being professional and strategic in your approach.

Build the case for Church partnership

Generally in society the level of faith literacy is very low, with little understanding of the nature and value of faith groups. You may need to state consistently that faith groups provide the largest voluntary cohort in the area, they probably employ the most youth and children workers, and studies [24] have shown they provide over 50 per cent of any social capital in the area (the social infrastructure of what make a community flourish). They are on the ground, with buildings and volunteers, and mostly pay their own way. Some unity movements have conducted very helpful faith audits that scope the work of the faith sector.

Learn the foreign language

If this is your first time in engaging with statutory authorities, you have just entered a foreign land where you need to learn the language and culture of civic

---

[24] Robert D Putnam, *Bowling Alone: The Collapse and Revival of American Community* (New York: Simon & Schuster, 2000).

organisations. The jargon is at times impenetrable, and the cultures are very complex. It's even worse if you are dealing with several authorities at the same time, with each one having its own distinctive language and culture. We need also to understand that Church culture and language to the outsider is just as bewildering.

The important thing is to keep asking questions, challenge the jargon and learn as fast as you can. Some unity groups talked about specific people who worked in the public sector in their congregations who greatly helped them in understanding the complexities involved.

Get the right attitude

It's very important to approach the engagement process with the right attitude. Most civic authorities expect local community groups to be negative, perhaps demanding, and at times critical. If you can be positive, appreciative, thankful and respectful, you will go a long way in enabling a long-term relationship to produce some significant fruit. A number of groups began with an event that invited the key civic leaders together to simply thank them for their service to the community. We don't have all the answers, we often haven't engaged in the past and we have much to learn about the process of building community; cultivating an attitude of humility will pay long-term dividends.

Serve; don't try to rule

The right attitude is fostered by a spirit of service to the community and its leaders. The Christian language sometimes used, 'conquering' or 'taking the land', has some negative connotations. We are here primarily to serve as Christ served, to build friendship, to seek the peace and prosperity of the place God has called us to.

You are part of a bigger picture

It's important to see ourselves as part of many others in the community. We are part of the wider faith community, and alongside many other community groups and associations who often do a tremendous work in serving the needs of an area. From sports clubs to scouting groups, from allotment associations to support groups, we must remember we are not the only show in town; we do have a unique contribution, but it's alongside others. We need to engage with not only the civic authorities but also the wider voluntary sector. We must at all times be humble, modest and self-effacing, taking our part in the larger picture and not seeking to exaggerate or boast.

One unity movement had to begin the conversation with their civic leaders with an apology for not engaging in the needs of the city and working with others over the previous twenty years. That humble beginning resulted in a very fruitful relationship over the next few years, where the churches played a significant role in the transformation of the city.

Remember, you are unique

Setting ourselves in a wider context then allows us to know the unique contribution we can make. We are a large voluntary force, with significant assets, serving in every neighbourhood of the area. Our faith is the driving force behind our activity, resulting in great commitment and ambition. It's vital we don't lose our unique identity and become just another type of third-sector organisation.

Faith sharing in a partly publicly funded project is appropriate when the conversation is initiated by those you serve. It can also be appropriate to advertise and invite people to other church activities you are running. Prayer is the underlying activity across all our areas of service, and the offer of prayer for individuals is often appreciated.

We must maintain our integrity to be ourselves and to be honest to our calling. The more you are able to prove your reliability with excellent outcomes, acquiring a proven track record in the process, the more this increases trust and allows you to have further freedom to express your faith-based uniqueness.

Don't forget the Church

The engagement process in the eyes of church members can appear strange, and may even be viewed by some as a distraction, or worse. As we engage with the civic authorities, we also need to engage with our local churches. We need over time to teach churches about the need to have a heart for the city, to seek its peace and prosperity. We need to encourage members to take up positions of responsibility in civic life, to highlight the Monday to Saturday callings of those already in our congregations who work in the public sector. It's good to pray regularly for those in authority in church services and to invite civic leaders to special occasions to interview them about their work and talk about their main priorities.

Be led by the Holy Spirit

Engagement is ultimately not about taking opportunities, being strategic and forming partnerships, it's about responding to the calling and direction of the Holy Spirit. If our plans and dreams are not soaked in prayer, led by divine guidance and enabled by the power of God, they will not succeed. Engagement is about prayer-walking, listening to Jesus about His dreams for our area, praying for the civic leaders, battling with the principalities and powers affecting our societies. All the effective unity movements that have pressed ahead with some outstanding civic engagement work have been founded, and fuelled, on prayer.

Under-promise and over-deliver

It's vital that we build up over time an impressive catalogue of effective sustainable community impact. We need to be trusted, but we only gain trust if we have the credibility regarding delivery on the commitments we have made. We do, of course, need to be imaginative and dream big visions, but it's vital we don't over-promise what we can deliver. We need to promise low but deliver higher than expectations.

It's a marathon, not a sprint

The dream of seeing our communities fundamentally changed over the next thirty years is not a quick fix. It will involve long-term commitment from churches and their leaders. There will be many times when you will want to give up, when the people you built great relationships with move on after a couple of years and you have to start all over again. When plans fail and partnerships break apart, we need to keep persevering and pressing on to what God has for us in the future. This is not a hit-and run-exercise, it involves a commitment that is constant and sustainable in order to see the purposes of God for our area.

Remember the poor

When the opportunities begin to grow and the options regarding service multiply, we need to make sure our greatest contribution is towards those who are the most vulnerable in our community. The pastoral care of the elderly, the homeless, the neglected and the abused is the bread and butter of what Church does best. It's the calling from Scripture to serve the least, the lost and the last, to feed the hungry, to clothe the naked and visit the prisoner (Matthew 25:34-45).

Focus on the big picture

Our engagement is not only about being part of the plans and actions of the statutory authorities, it's about being part of the greater purposes of God. We are drawn into God's mission to this world to bring about the establishment of His kingdom, to see a new heaven and new earth, a renewed neighbourhood and transformed borough, a changed city. This is His work and we are invited to be part of it; we are greatly privileged to be drawn into His purposes for creation.

Chapter 9
The New Future

I hope you are excited about the growth, scope and impact of unity movements across the country. What isn't really covered in this book is that what God is doing in the UK, He is also doing across the world.

In my own travels, it been incredible to meet city leaders from Japan, Brazil, Africa, Australia, Pacific islands, America, India, Canada and Europe. Although expressed differently in each culture, the values of relational unity, sustained prayer and coordinated and strategic mission are common to all. We can trace some of the main influencing factors, but by and large this has been a grass roots movement and, I believe, the closest thing I have seen to a move of God across the world. This is not only beginning in the West in Berlin, Dallas and Toronto, but also in Mumbai, Jakarta and Chennai. No one church, ministry or denomination has ultimately fuelled this; this is not a fad or the latest fashion, since it's been going in some cities for over twenty-five years.

When the Church of God begins to see itself as one body across a city or town, when it begins to pray and relate in close friendship across denominational lines, when its ordinary members begin to see themselves as God's agents of change and form relational and strategic networks across the spheres of society, when Christians begin to own and love the places they are sent to and develop an all-encompassing transformational vision, then something very significant is happening.

Is God fundamentally reforming the Church across the world in cities and towns, to begin a new wave of His mission to the world? If social, cultural and spiritual kingdom transformation begins to affect and change cities and towns, you are beginning to change a nation. If you begin to change nations, you begin to change the world.

The keys to all this are the basics we have been talking about. Loving relational unity, together with sustained prayer, and engaging in strategic and coordinated mission produces much fruit. Or to put it another way, loving God and loving the body of Christ, resulting in a greater love for the places God has called us to bless, is creating a simple but profound dynamic. How this is outworked, in specific places using specific strategies, will be multifaceted. Each city and town we have charted in our own country is working things out differently; how much more will this happen across the world? When I meet with city leaders from very different cultures, countries and backgrounds, working out this transformational calling, I am energised by the uniqueness of each context, but it's all very familiar. They all love God and they love the body of Christ and they really love their places.

As we begin to look to the future, I am amazed at the potential of what we have spoken about. It feels as if getting the Church to the stage where friendships are forming across a place, and unity is growing, with sustained prayer happening, and then some joined-up mission is being undertaken, is just stage one of God's missional agenda. What we have now, as good as it is, is not the goal; it's just the start. Perhaps this is why Christ above all things in the garden prayed for His Church to be in unity, in relationship together, as He was with the Father. The problem is, it has taken some time to get to stage one. But now we are here, in many places across the world, the future is extremely exciting, because it opens up numerous possibilities which were once unthinkable.

The most significant untapped potential is the releasing, training, encouraging and blessing of ordinary Christians in the spheres of life. When a Christian teacher sees herself as a city-changer and begins to meet and pray with other teachers, assistants, support staff and senior educationalists across a city on a regular basis over a long period of time, something deeply theological and very strategic is starting to happen. If she is encouraged in her calling, supported through the hard times and given the resources to be the very best teacher she can be, then we will begin to see children better supported and educated. If she was then part of a smaller core team with some key policymakers who begin to dream of a better education system across the city, who begin to pray for some significant changes that would benefit children and teachers, then something special is happening. If that smaller core team began to develop a vision for education, working alongside the local authority or major educational trust, then the dreams and plans could begin to have some traction.

If a Christian business owner began to feel supported and validated in his role by his local church, if he joined in prayer with other Christian business owners across the town, if they began to connect intentionally with the local business forums and started to develop with them a vision for business across the town, could they begin to see some kingdom transformation producing more employment, and more investment? If this was replicated in the arts, health, politics, local government, sports and media, could we begin to see greater levels of kingdom transformation? However this is worked out in each context, it certainly begins to open up very imaginative possibilities.

There does create some serious challenges, though, if we are to fully realise this vision, and we will have to see some significant changes to how we do things.

Some key challenges/opportunities

1. The role of the local church leader is paramount in enabling this to happen. If we continue to press ahead with a church-centred/my patch/my people approach, where success is determined by how many people we have on a Sunday morning, the size of the building and the ministry, then we will struggle to see the bigger transformation vision. Christians in the church will continue to live dualistic segregated lives, where Sunday, the midweek small group and their area of service in church will take emotional and spiritual precedence over their work and family lives. This must be turned on its head; as pastors we must see our people as God's gifts to their families, to their

neighbourhoods and the wider city. Our role is to enable them in the work of service; we must become their greatest supporters, and not they ours. We should be providing training, encouragement, support, motivation to be the city-changers they are called to be, to be the best neighbours that street has ever had, to be the best of friends, the most loving marriage partners and parents. This change is fundamental to how pastors see themselves and how they are trained to do their role. This change, then, involves not only the pastor but the training college and the denomination.

2. The denominations and national Christian organisations are also implicated by this move of God. As church leaders and church members increasingly see themselves called to serve and build locally in cities and towns, if God is unveiling a biblical priority to begin to see places transformed, then this has implications for those who view things from a top-down national perspective. Let me give you some examples:

   a. It can be very disruptive to a vibrant unity movement when some denominations and streams move their leaders around from city to city on a regular basis to benefit the needs of the denomination; it disturbs relationships and can undermine significant city-based working. Denominations and streams will need to begin to be empathetic and respectful to the ministry of the body of Christ across a city. This not only makes sense for the work in that city but also the denomination, since it is generally accepted that church growth is more often than not more successful the longer a leader stays in place over the long-term.

b.   It is always irritating, disrespectful and sometimes undermining when national Christian organisations decide without any consultation to enter a city or town with their latest ministry which they are rolling out nationally. If a city or town has a joined-up, organised unity movement, it is honouring and, to be honest, common sense to begin conversations with the pastors of that city. National ministries have much to offer and add to the ministry of a place, but, moving into the future, this must be more and more about invitation than imposition if we are to progress.

c.   Underlining this change in perspective by the national towards the city level, we begin to understand that perhaps something more profound is happening here. Is the local meant to serve the national, or the national meant to serve the local? Sometimes it can be a weakness in the nature of powerful national institutions and denominations that they can become self-serving entities in themselves; the challenge of the city perspective is to reverse that paradigm. Surely the call to be part of the social, cultural and spiritual transformation of a city or town is as important as or more important than the national needs of a denomination or a Christian charity? The national can play a huge role in supporting those on the ground. One very creative way to make this paradigm change is to have joined-up conversations about the use of redundant church buildings across a city. Could we move to a time when denominations begin a conversation with unity movements before they close and sell a building in a town, to see if that building could be used by others in the kingdom to effect more mission to the area? Even if that building has to be sold, could other churches in the wider body of Christ be given first refusal? This paradigm change could be effected in other areas of ministry such as training, Child Protection Services, legal support. Why are we duplicating so many support services carried out by multiple denominations, when we could be much more cooperative, save more money and release more resources for the kingdom? The call to strategic and coordinated unity is not just a call to cities and towns but also to national denominations and organisations. The call to a kingdom mentality must also be heard and lived in all the body of Christ.

3. The challenge of resources is a future area of need for funding and supporting these wonderful unity movements. Local churches tend to focus their funds on supporting the ministry of their own church, their denomination, and then often give to other national and international needs. If the vision for their city or

town is growing, if their people are beginning to affect the cultural spheres, then financial and time resources will need to be directed towards this most vital of ministries. This is also a challenge for national Christian charities, trusts and philanthropists to begin to see the strategic importance of this work and support it accordingly.

In summary, looking at what God is doing across the world, we are seeing a pattern develop in how cities and towns could change over the next twenty to thirty years. Let's recap and look at the essential steps that need to be taken:

- **Growing city focus.** Transformation of our places will only happen as church and other Christian leaders begin to view their ministry from the perspective of the city and not just their local church or denominational agenda.

- **Relational unity.** No one church, agency or individual will enable cultural, social and spiritual transformation. Churches and key Christian leaders in the cultural and social spheres need to build strong relationships and work together.

- **Sustained united prayer.** The transformation of our places is ultimately an act of God through the establishment of the kingdom. United prayer must be at the centre of all that is undertaken, responding to the Spirit's initiative and taking authority over the places God has called us to.

- **Developing growing missional churches.** There is no shortcut to the progress of transformation; we will need to plant and grow more and more healthy churches, who incarnate their ministry in the locality and grow through conversion.

- **Churches growing whole-life disciples.** Growing and planting more churches in itself is not enough to see transformation. To affect the cultural and social spheres of an area, church members will need to be inspired, trained and released to be kingdom people in their places of work and neighbourhoods. Church institutions and their leaders can never sufficiently affect the cultural and social fabric of their cities; they do, however, have in their congregations the people who can bring about transformation.

- **Support of Christians in the cultural and social spheres.** To affect the cultural and social spheres of an area, Christians in those spheres will have to be enabled to join together in regular prayer, support and training. (Health, education, arts, media, council, business, etc.) Not only must unity between church leaders be grown to effect transformation, but also unity of spirit and purpose between Christians in the cultural spheres and the cultural sphere networks and the Church unity network. God is joining up all things to bring about an all-things transformation.

- **Emergence of Christian public leadership.** Arising from the support of Christians in the cultural and social spheres, it will increasingly be important to see raised-up Christians who can become key public leaders, especially in government, business and media contexts.

- **Public- and private-sector engagement towards the renewal of civil society.** For churches working together in unity for the transformation of their areas, it is vital they work in partnership with other third-sector organisations, in the public and private sectors. A new spirit of partnership must develop between churches and social institutions such as: local government, cultural centres, third-sector charities, schools, businesses, police and health bodies – those public and private bodies that are working towards the common good.

- **Special focus on poverty reduction.** With so many possibilities for service, churches and Christian agencies will need to work together in unity and primarily focus on those who are the most vulnerable in society, affected by material and relational poverty.

It must be stressed that this is a long-term work; this is not a short-time burst of activity. Cities are complex organisms, with long histories and ingrained cultures; however, the gospel tells us that Christ will draw all things to Himself (Ephesians 1:10) and if His prayer for unity is heard and lived out, and if God's people can fully join Him in His mission, then over time resurrection will happen, transformation will come about. This is essentially a generational commitment of sacrifice and service to a place. Any movement of transformation across a city or town will be built on previous generations who have prayed and worked all their lives – we all stand on the ministry of others – and then the baton will be passed on to another generation, and year by year, decade by decade, God's kingdom will grow and become a harvest of social, cultural and spiritual transformation.

I would like to end this account of this move of God across our cities and towns to pay tribute to the work of unity leaders in numerous places across the UK. It has been my privilege to meet many of them and to become friends over the last few years. I have a huge respect for them and their ministries; alongside the demanding needs of the local church, they have put themselves forward to gather people together, to do the hard work of relationship-forming and mission-leading. They won't have any titles, additional income or prestige, but are the true bishops, apostles and prophets to the city. They have put their heads above the parapet, they have taken responsibility, they have paid the price and they probably won't receive what has been promised (Hebrews 11:39). All of us should be inspired by their ministries and respond by loving God, loving our brothers and sisters, and loving our places. If you are a Christian businessman or woman, be inspired by these people, set up a business network across your town. It you are an artist, gather others around you to begin to make a difference. If you are a church leader with little going on in effective unity, then find one other leader and simply meet and pray with them regularly; start to prayer-walk the town and ask God for a word for the future.

The vision of Gather has simply been to see an effective unity movement of God's people in church and across every village, town, city, borough and island in the UK.

This book is telling the story of where this vision is up to at the moment, the lessons learned and key values identified. But this is part of a much larger international development with so much potential yet to be released. Is this a major reformation of the Church? History will tell us, but it's certainly extensive, and very exciting.

Further Information

(All websites accessed 6th July 2017.)

Gather: www.gather.global
Gather is a national network of over 130 unity movements across the UK. It exists to network cities and towns where relational, prayerful and missional unity is happening and to encourage it to begin in places where it isn't yet happening.

The Evangelical Alliance: www.eauk.org
The largest and oldest body representing the UK's 2 million evangelical Christians, they seek to bring Christians together by helping them listen to, and be heard by, the government, media and society. The EA has been a core supporter of Gather, seeking to support unity movements across the UK without owning or controlling what God is doing. The EA has two very good websites. The first is called The Great Commission and provides resources on evangelism. It is available at https://greatcommission.co.uk. The second provides resources on developing public leaders and is available at https://thepublicleader.com.

Redeeming our Communities: https://roc.uk.com
ROC's main aim is to bring about community transformation by creating strategic partnerships between statutory agencies, voluntary groups and churches. These partnerships form new volunteer-led projects that address a variety of social needs.

London Institute of Contemporary Christianity: www.licc.org.uk
Empowering Christians to make a difference for Christ in our Monday-to-Saturday lives, helping church leaders equip their church communities to do it, and fuelling a movement to reach and renew our nation.

Cinnamon Network: www.cinnamonnetwork.co.uk
Cinnamon Network aims to make it as easy as possible for local churches to transform their communities by reaching out and building life-giving relationships with those in greatest need.

Churches Together in England: http://www.cte.org.uk
Churches Together in England is an organisation bringing together the vast majority of denominations in England. It seeks a deepening of communion with Christ and with one another, and proclaims the Gospel together by common witness and service.

World Prayer Centre: www.worldprayer.org.uk
WPC have a coordinating role across the movement for prayer in the UK and provide prayer resources and information and run a range of prayer events. They have

been a great support to prayer movements in cities and towns across the UK.

HOPE: www.hopetogether.org.uk

HOPE brings churches together in mission. The goal is to see individuals and communities in villages, towns and cities throughout the UK transformed by Jesus' love. HOPE has significantly helped to establish unity movements in a number of cities and towns over the last ten years.

City to City: www.citytocity.org

City to City are about transformation. They recognise that to achieve transformation, Christians need to get involved in every sphere of society. They seek to initiate conversations across the spheres of society to bring about opportunities for change and transformation.

Movement Day: www.movementday.com

Challenging, inspiring and catalysing the advancement of the gospel movements across the world.

City Changers: http://citychanger.org

Global City Changers Movement is an extension of the Doxa Deo Church in Pretoria led by Alan Platt. It seeks to mobilise the church-based Christian community in different spheres of society for the transformation of cities globally.